THE
ESSENTIAL
RUNNER

THE
ESSENTIAL
RUNNER

JOHN HANC

LYONS & BURFORD, PUBLISHERS

Copyright © 1994 by John Hanc

ALL RIGHTS RESERVED. No part of this book may be reproduced in any manner without the express written consent of the publisher, except in the case of brief excerpts in critical reviews and articles. All inquiries should be addressed to: Lyons & Burford, 31 West 21 Street, New York, NY 10010.

Printed in the United States of America

Illustrations by Manuel F. Cheo

Design by Howard P. Johnson

10 9 8 7 6 5 4 3

Hanc, John.
    The essential runner / John Hanc.
        p.   cm.
    Includes bibliographical references and index.
    ISBN 1-55821-289-2
    1. Running.   2. Physical fitness.   I. Title.
    GV1061.H316   1994
    796.42—dc20   93-48440
                                                                        CIP

This book is not intended to be a substitute for medical advice. Anyone beginning a running program should receive clearance from their doctor, especially those who are over 45 years old, have a family history of coronary artery disease, or have any of the other risk factors commonly associated with coronary artery disease, such as high blood pressure, high cholesterol levels, diabetes, obesity or cigarette smoking.

CONTENTS

ACKNOWLEDGMENTS

Many people helped get this book on its feet. In fact, I had an informal advisory board of medical and running experts without whose generous input *The Essential Runner* would have been essentially impossible: Nancy Clark, R.D., author and nationally known sports nutritionist; Bob Cook, owner of The Runner's Edge athletic footwear store in Farmingdale, NY; Larry Davidson, a coach and consultant to the American Heart Association; Edward Fryman, D.P.M., medical director of the *Newsday* Long Island Marathon; John Peters, M.D., a marathoner and cardiologist at North Shore University Hospital; Mike Polansky, president of the Plainview-Old Bethpage Road Runners Club; pediatrician Reuben Reiman, M.D.; Andres Rodriguez, M.D., medical director of the New York City Marathon; Thomas Scandalis, D.O., chief of sports medicine at the New York College of Osteopathic Medicine/New York Institute of Technology in Old Westbury, NY;

and, finally, the late George Sheehan, M.D., the philosopher-king of runners everywhere.

I'd also like to thank three friends who helped in the actual research and writing of this book: writers Don Mogelefsky and Paul Hertneky, for their special contributions to Chapters 5 and 7, respectively; and Zachary Miller, my meticulous research assistant who helped prepare the appendices.

Some of the material in this book has appeared in one form or another in various publications I've written for over the past decade. First and foremost among these is *Newsday*. I've been writing about running and fitness for the Long Island and New York City editions of this newspaper for nearly a decade. I'd like to thank those who gave me the opportunities, and from whom I've learned much about being a journalist. Paul Ballot, A.J. Carter, Tony Castineiras, Bob Herzog, Tim Layden, Gary Schwartz and John Quinn of *Newsday* Sports deserve special mention.

Similar thanks to the folks at *Runner's World* magazine, where I have been a contributing writer for about three years; and particularly to its executive editor, Amby Burfoot—a great runner, a great writer, and a true gentleman.

I'd also like to thank Gordon Bakoulis, Stan Kramberg—my biggest fan (outside of my mom)—and Raleigh Mayer of the New York Road Runners Club for their help and encouragement. Also thanks to my agent, Julian Bach, my confidante, Lee. R. Schreiber, and Peter Burford and Amy Young at Lyons & Burford, for being so pleasant to work with.

My various training partners deserve credit—not just for the pleasurable companionship they've offered me over the years, but for their knowledge and experience, much of which was incorporated into this book: Patti Coyle, Bill Gilmartin, Doug Hynes, Greg Karl, Marty Linksy, Bill Prewitt, Mike Sharrer and Bud Rourke.

To the two women in my life: my mom, Dolores Hanc, and my wife, Donna, whom I could have listed as a contributor—so great a help was she on this project—but who deserves a special place on this page, as she does in my life.

Finally, to all those who run: Have fun. See you on the roads.

—John Hanc
Farmingdale, New York
October, 1993

FOREWORD

AMBY BURFOOT

EXECUTIVE EDITOR, *RUNNER'S WORLD*

Every runner is a beginning runner. The young runner is a beginner. The middle-aged man worried about his spreading waistline is a beginner. The 52-year-old woman whose kids have finally left for college is a beginner. So is the injured runner making a comeback, the college student who wants to add aerobic exercise to his weight training, and the executive whose workload has finally slackened off enough to allow him to return to marathoning.

I am a beginner too. As I write these words, I have just recently begun to train for my first marathon in five years. Twenty-five years ago I won the Boston Marathon, and I've run more or less continually ever since. But today I feel like a beginning runner again.

I wouldn't have it any other way. The beginning runner is the luckiest of runners. Ahead lies a road of unknown length and adventures, a road inevitably filled with challenges and obstacles. But that road is also filled, I have learned, with unexpected pleasures and unimagined successes.

Beginning runners almost always achieve far more than they ever thought possible. Who ever believed they could run all the way to the end of the block and back without stopping? Or four times around the local high school track? Or from the Verrazano-Narrows Bridge, through the five boroughs of New York City, to the finish of the New York City Marathon in Central Park?

Yet an incredibly high percentage of runners who attempt these feats succeed at them. The New York City Road Runners Club, organizer of the marathon, maintains an accurate accounting of all starters and all finishers. Each November, more than 25,000 runners begin the marathon —young French women; middle-aged Nebraskans; flinty, 70-year-old white hairs from New Zealand. And each November, a startling 95 percent of these runners complete the arduous and hilly 26.2-mile course. An equally high percentage is apparently astonished by their success. Trust me. I know about these things, because many of them send their personal stories to me at Runner's World, hoping that they might be published.

I can't publish these stories, or at least not very many of them, but I read them all, and I must admit to being impressed. These are stories filled with the humblest of beginnings and the most dramatic of endings. The overweight, the cigarette smokers, the drug and alcohol addicts begin running, and almost before they know it, they are crossing the marathon finish line with tears streaming down their cheeks. Time after time, the stories end with the line: "It was the happiest and proudest day of my life."

Even after the marathon, the runners keep writing to

me. Having accomplished the seemingly impossible, many of them press on to tackle other major challenges in their lives. They work up the nerve to finally get divorced or to leave an old, dead-end job. They ask for an overdue promotion at work. They decide to go back to college. "Once you've conquered a marathon," these letter writers say, "nothing else seems quite so hard to imagine as it did before."

Indeed, after all these years, I've learned that finishing the marathon—or even 5 or 10 miles, if that's as far as you choose to go—isn't just an athletic achievement. It's a state of mind; a state of mind that says anything is possible.

The athletic shoe company Nike is best known today for its "Just Do It" slogan. But a few years ago, Nike was championing a different phrase: "There Is No Finish Line." That's exactly what every marathoner learns—that the lessons gleaned from marathoning spill over into all other parts of one's life. And it's exactly what I've learned from more than 30 years of running.

In 1968, at the stripling age of 22, I won the Boston Marathon. No one ever deserved to win Boston more than I did, because no one had ever trained harder or lived a life more devoted to marathon success. But that devotion— the training and the mental preparation—is not important. My recipe for winning the Boston Marathon matters little to me today. What matters is that I have cultivated a certain attitude about running. I look upon each day, each year, and each phase of my running career as a whole new beginning—a beginning that can only lead to regeneration, greater self-knowledge, and exciting new horizons.

The same year I won Boston, I also won a Thanksgiving Day Turkey Trot in Manchester, Connecticut. I went on to win the same race eight more times in the next decade. My last Turkey Trot victory was in 1977. You must wonder why I'm boring you with details about a relatively unimportant race. Simple. Because Manchester is anything but unimportant to me. In fact, it has become far more important to me than winning Boston, competing in the Olympic trials, or any of the many other big races I've run in my life. You see even though I don't win Manchester anymore, I'm still running in it. Every Thanksgiving morning for the past 30 years, I've lined up at the start of the Turkey Trot, and every Thanksgiving morning for the last 30 years, I've reached the finish at the end of the Turkey Trot. One year I had pneumonia and had to jog near the back of the pack. One year I pulled a leg muscle in midcourse and had to limp to the end. At my best, I run minutes slower than I did two decades ago. But every year I run, 30 years in a row. If there is a finish line, I haven't seen it yet. And I hope I never will.

Woody Allen once said that 90 percent of life is just showing up (or 95 percent, or 99, depending on where you read the quip). Someone at Nike ought to give Allen a job writing ad copy. What Allen said about life is even more true about running. At least 99 percent of running is just showing up, getting out there and putting one foot in front of the other.

Still, you need a road map to make sure you don't get lost, and that's exactly what John Hanc has provided in the pages that follow. John has been there himself, both as a runner and as a running writer, and he understands the turf well. Whether explaining shoes, nutrition, interval training, or marathon preparation, John knows the sport and how to convey its essential truths.

If you've picked up this book, you're obviously interested in becoming a beginning runner, whether for the first time or the fiftieth. Good for you. With John as your guide, you can't go wrong. There's only one thing John can't do: He can't run down the road for you. The road has your name on it and no one else's. Lucky you.

INTRODUCTION

Max Popper was feeling mighty low. The year was 1975, and Max had just retired from his job as a municipal engineer for the city of New York. Now, faced with the rest of his life, he grew increasingly depressed. "I had not prepared for retirement," he recalled. "I became nuts for two years. I was thinking of silly things—even of suicide. It was that bad."

To help his dad beat the blues, Popper's son Andrew suggested that they go out for a run. Max declined, but finally, under pressure, the elder Popper joined Andrew for a run through Central Park. He put one foot in front of the other—and hasn't stopped since.

Popper went on to become one of the top senior runners in America. In 1986, at age 83, he set records at every distance from 5 to 25 kilometers. He knocked a full 2 minutes off the half-marathon (13.1 miles) record that year, registering a time of 1 hour, 50 minutes—a respectable mark for people half his age.

But how fast Max runs seems to be less important than the fact that he runs, period. "People don't give a damn about my times," he admits. "When they see the oldest runner, it's an inspiration." Indeed, Max invariably seems to draw the biggest applause in any event he competes in. Running luminaries such as New York Road Runners Club president Fred Lebow and the late author and cardiologist Dr. George Sheehan have called him a hero.

Maybe it's his dapper looks: With a full head of hair and his trim, 120-pound figure, he could pass for a man 20 years younger. Or maybe it's because they think Max knows some great secret of life and longevity. "People ask me what I eat, how I train. They even ask me about my sex life." That, says Max, is nobody's business. But what I can tell you is that, outside of his genetic makeup, there's no mystery to Max's success; but there is something to be learned. At age 90, Max teaches us about the benefits of running and physical fitness; about how a running regimen, combined with a proper diet and healthy life-style, can dramatically change the way we look, feel, perform, work, and live.

The medical community has slowly and cautiously reached these same conclusions. But their studies and statistics, although important and impressive, can't compare with the simple, living proof offered by people like Max. "I'm a confirmation of the promise of running," he says. "The promise that it will add meaningful, active years to your life."

You don't have to run the marathon to discover what Max Popper has. You don't have to run very fast, or very long, or every day. You don't even have to run. There are other fine cardiovascular activities—swimming, cycling, cross-country skiing, even walking—that can help you achieve similar benefits; activities that many runners incorporate into their training programs.

But, as Max himself found out, few are as accessible, inexpensive, and satisfying as running. That is why today, 20 years after Frank Shorter won the marathon in the 1972 Olympics and helped start the so-called running boom, thousands of people each year are starting, and hundreds of thousands more continue. What keeps them at it? Probably some of the same things that keep Max logging his daily miles—all the way, we hope, into the next century.

"When you have that running spirit, you look forward to life," says Max. "I firmly believe that I wouldn't have lived as long or as happily as I have without running."

So what can it do for you? Improve your tennis game—or change your life? Maybe a bit of both.

WHAT HAPPENS
TO YOUR BODY
WHEN YOU RUN

You put one foot in front of the other and start to move faster and faster and faster. Now you're running. You may start huffing and puffing. You'll probably break a sweat. You'll definitely understand why they call it a workout.

Why? What's going on inside? You don't need to be a medical expert, but you should be aware of what happens to your body when you run—what you do to it and for it.

Cardiologist and marathon runner John Peters uses a car analogy to explain to schoolchildren how the cardio-vascular system works, which means that maybe it's simple enough for us adults too. "Think of the heart as the engine, because it's really what makes the body go," says Peter. "The oxygen is like gasoline, which you get from your lungs—the gas tank. For your car to work properly, you need clean tubes and hoses—these are your arteries, which have to be open and clear in order to deliver the oxygen from the heart to the muscles. Finally, when the entire process works correctly, the tires spin—your feet move."

To take this neat little analogy one step further: When you push the accelerator pedal of your car, the engine responds by working harder. When you begin to run or engage in any strenuous exercise, your body responds in the same way. First, your heart rate goes up. How far and how fast depends on your level of conditioning and how much stress you're placing on the heart. Any time you ask your body to do work—whether it's to row a boat, push a lawn mower, or run a marathon—the muscles that must respond to the task demand more oxygen. And the only way they're going to get it is through an increased flow of blood away from other parts of the body—where it's not as important at the moment—to where the action is: the legs, in the case of running.

Now keep in mind that the function of the heart is to perform as a pump. When you go harder and faster, it pumps harder and faster, pumping out six times the amount of blood when you're running as when you're at rest. In order to "shunt" the blood to where it's needed, your heart has to pump faster, so that each time it contracts it pumps harder, sending more blood coursing through the arteries.

It sounds like you're asking an awful lot of the old ticker. But it's nothing a healthy heart can't handle. "Stress is one thing," says Peters. "Strain is another." Remember—the heart is a muscle, and like any other muscle, it requires more blood when it's asked to do more work.

The heart receives its blood supply from the coronary arteries. As demand increases during exercise, the blood flow should increase too—provided there are no blockages in the coronary arteries. Such blockages—or occlusions—

could be a precursor to angina and heart attacks. For this reason, it is always recommended that individuals who are starting a running or any kind of exercise program get a checkup first. This means you too, especially if you're over 40 and/or have a family history of heart disease. Chances are, your physician will not only give you the okay to exercise but will also encourage you. Although there may be some quibbling in the medical community about how much and to what extent, there's no doubt about the beneficial effects of running on the heart and lungs. We'll examine those benefits in a moment.

First, let's get back to that body in motion. We've talked about how running helps strengthen the heart muscle by forcing it to work harder. But in the middle of a run, you're usually not aware of your heartbeat. What you do hear is the sound of your own breathing getting heavier and more labored as you go along—especially if you're just starting out or going harder than you should.

At rest, most of us use only 40 to 50 percent of our total lung capacity. But as we start to run, our oxygen demand increases and we start taking deeper and deeper breaths. The more we do, the more lung tissue we recruit to do the job. In other words, we tap into more of our pulmonary potential.

So here you are, running along, and all your systems are on full "go." The heart's pumping away, the blood's flowing, the legs are moving, the lungs are expanding. It sounds like you're taxing the body dangerously, pushing it close to some kind of overload. Actually, the opposite is true. Running helps us use our bodies to their full capabilities—capabilities that *should* be utilized. You've heard the phrase "use it or lose it." It most certainly applies to the use of your cardiopulmonary system. Unless you give the body the opportunity to exercise regularly, its full potential as the most efficient long-distance machine ever devised by nature will be lost.

"It's like having a car that can run 140 miles an hour, but you only drive it around at 35," says Peters, using his favorite analogy once again. "Eventually you won't be able to drive that car at 140."

Your body wasn't designed to do 140. But neither was it supposed to spend most of its time in a chair, on the couch, or in the front seat of a motorized vehicle. This is why so many people respond so well to running and exercise programs. For the first time in their lives—or at least since high school or boot camp—they're being all that they can be.

The runners you see on the track or on the roads near your home aren't doing things they were never capable of. They're doing exactly what their bodies are supposed to be doing, which gives new meaning to the phrase "born to run." I think you'll find that once you're into your program, running will feel like the most natural thing in the world—which it may be.

WHAT RUNNING CAN DO FOR YOUR BODY

We've talked about what running does *to* you. Now let's look at what it does *for* you:

1. Running helps lower your blood pressure by maintaining the elasticity of your arteries. In order to handle the increased blood flow that occurs when you run, the arteries must be able to expand and contract to a greater degree than they normally would. That's important. "If the artery isn't flexible, moving blood through it is like trying to drive water through a lead pipe," explains Peters. "The pressure gets higher. Whereas, if you drive water through a rubber hose, which can expand, the pressure stays the same." The hose won't burst, but the pipe will. Do you want hoses or pipes for your arteries? Running helps keep them elastic, thereby helping to keep your normal blood pressure low.

2. **Running maximizes your lungs' potential, keeping them strong.** We talked about how your lungs are forced to recruit more tissue as you take in deeper and deeper breaths as you run. Without such exercise, the 50 percent of the lung potential that normally doesn't get used will vanish—again, the "use it or lose it" principle at work. And work—in the form of running and other aerobic exercise—is what you need to maintain the lung power you've got. If you're under 50 years old and haven't damaged your lungs through heavy smoking, running will help the lungs maintain their full potential. If you're over 50, you may have already lost some of that potential lung power, so it may take you a bit longer to feel comfortable. Don't despair: Some people have been able to recover their full lung power. Talk about a second wind!

3. **Running strengthens your heart and helps prevent heart attacks.** Yes, it's true, despite what happened to the late, great Jim Fixx (see the section on Myths and Commonly Asked Questions About Running). Remember, the heart is a muscle like any other. Without exercise, it will atrophy—waste away—getting weaker and less efficient.

Running is one of the best exercises—if not the best—for the heart and blood vessels: the cardiovascular system. The demands of this continuous-motion, large-muscle exercise help keep this most vital muscle strong and working efficiently. How efficiently? Consider that the heart of an inactive person beats 36,000 more times a day than the heart of someone who's fit.

As for the vascular part, we mentioned earlier how running helps keep the coronary arteries open so that they can supply increased blood flow to the heart, which, in turn, can increase its pumping action to supply more blood to the lower body. Blocked and closed arteries cause heart attacks. Although this is partially a function of diet and hereditary factors, exercise can help; by keeping the arterial highways open and the blood flowing smoothly, it's an important part of the formula for preventing the nation's number-one killer.

4. Running gives you more energy in your daily life. Yes, I know it sounds like a claim for some miracle food product. But ask any of your friends who run and they'll tell you how much more energetic they feel as a result of their training.

Here's why: Regular exercise makes your body function more efficiently, not just when you're exercising, but all day long. You'll be able to do more work while expending the same or less energy. You'll be able to work longer, because you'll have more energy available. And you won't be as tired at the end of a day's work, because you will have been able to perform the same tasks using less energy.

This point was made dramatically in a public-service announcement for a local hospital in New York. First we heard the sound of a marathoner's heart as he ran a race: It went bump-bump-bump. Then we heard the sound of an out-of-shape person's heart as he walked around the block.

Same thing. The point was that the runner could do more with the same amount of energy, because his heart was stronger and more efficient.

5. Running helps you lose weight. This is the most common reason people start running. And there is no question that running will burn calories, if you do it for a long enough time. That's an important "if" for beginners, who may be running only 15 or 20 minutes when they start. Sorry to say, but that's not going to burn off six slices of pizza.

Once you get up to 45 to 60 minutes of running, you'll be burning lots of calories and fat. Combined with a proper diet, this should result in significant weight loss—weight that you'll keep off, as long as you keep up your running. But it's going to happen gradually, so be patient. And don't use your first few weeks of running as an excuse to pig out.

Other benefits from running vary from individual to individual. For example, once you're on a running program, you may find that you sleep better, that your appetite is better, that you feel more relaxed. These are all "quality of life" benefits. They're rooted, Peters believes, in the physiological benefits we've discussed here. "The key in terms of fitness is efficiency," he says. "Running helps the entire system run more efficiently: heart, lungs, arteries. Those benefits are 100 percent attainable by almost anyone."

WHAT RUNNING CAN DO
FOR YOUR MIND

To nonrunners, the notion that pounding the pavement for mile after mile leads to anything resembling pleasure is preposterous. Among runners, the opinions are divided as well. Many claim to have reached euphoric states during or after a run. But for just as many other runners, the notion is absurd. As one veteran commented to me, "The only high I get from running comes later, when I get home and have a post-race Scotch."

The truth behind the so-called runner's high is still elusive. The term *endorphins* was originally used as a generic label for a whole class of chemicals secreted by the pituitary gland of the brain. Working together with a smaller class of compounds called *enkephalins*, these chemicals mimic some of the properties of opiate narcotics and function as a sort of natural painkiller. Of the 15 types that have been identified, one is called *betaendorphins*. It is the combination of these betaendorphins and enkephalins that may alleviate the pain of vigorous exercise.

The way this works was described to me by one researcher as a sort of mental Drano. In simplest terms, the substances open up the neurons—the communication links—in your nervous system. "It's like unstopping a clogged up drain," he explained. "What flows through are communication impulses that send a signal to counteract or inhibit pain."

This process is not restricted to running. In fact, betaendorphin release has been demonstrated to occur during acupuncture—a particular nerve is hit that triggers the pituitary gland—and in combat situations in which soldiers who had lost limbs felt no pain due to the anesthetic effect of these substances. Some scientists also suspect that there are those who have taught themselves to secrete endorphins—which may explain such feats as walking over hot coals barefoot.

All this may give you the impression that running is about as much fun as having those hot coals dropped down the back of your shirt. Not so. While biochemists continue to debate the relationship of endorphins and euphoria among runners, psychologists are using running as a successful treatment for clinical depression. In fact, one team of researchers concluded that it works just as well as traditional psychotherapy.

In another major study, runners were found to be less tense, less depressed, less fatigued, less confused, and more vigorous than nonrunners. These findings were replicated in a 1984 study of women runners. What's more, this research indicated that beginners and lower-mileage runners seem to get the same psychological benefits as more advanced competitors. Those women who ran 24 miles a week—an average of just 3½ miles a day—scored better than anyone else on all measures of mood and scored just as high as marathoners in their feelings of vigor.

Other studies have shown significant reductions in tension, anxiety, anger, and hostility among runners. This is consistent with the oft-repeated idea that running is a sort of "natural tranquilizer."

Although the research into runner's high and endorphins is inconclusive, the evidence on how running affects your head suggests that we runners—though not as high as kites—are at least more "up" than most people in an average traffic jam. "As a runner, you have a level of anxiety that's likely to be lower than that felt by the general population," concluded one expert. "In other words, running seems able to make you a happy person."

So don't go out there waiting to feel the effects of betaendorphins. Go out there and just feel good.

Will running make you a better golfer or tennis player? Will it improve your performance on the basketball court, the baseball diamond, the soccer field, the gridiron? No. Or at least, not directly.

As any coach will tell you, the way to improve in any sport is to practice and develop the skills that are specific to that sport. That makes sense, but there are other factors in athletics: strength, speed, stamina. And that's where a running regimen can help. By building your endurance and improving your stamina, you will be able to stay fresher and, therefore, play better for longer periods of time. That's why so many athletes incorporate distance running into their training regimens. Boxers have been doing their roadwork since the days of bare-knuckle fighters. Baseball players are more recent recruits, but now many if not most major leaguers put in some miles before games or during the off-season.

Running builds something along with endurance: confidence. That is one reason that two-time Olympic gold medal wrestler John Smith—regarded by some as the best American grappler in history—runs 3 to 4 miles a day. "When I step on the mat," he told a writer, "I know I'm prepared. When I have that knowledge, there are times I feel unbeatable."

Let's look at how running can help improve your endurance, confidence, and performance in one particular—and particularly popular—sport: tennis.

Jimmy Connors was reportedly an avid runner during

his career—a career that lasted a long, long time. Any relationship? You bet. Chris Evert found the same thing: When she added running to her workouts, her stamina—and her tennis game—improved. And thousands of less-gifted tennis players have found the same thing.

"You don't play tennis to get in shape," says Brad Patterson of the American Tennis Industry Foundation. "You get in shape to play tennis." Of course, tennis itself is a challenging fitness activity. But if you want to play better and longer, running should be part of your training program. "Running won't improve your backhand," Patterson says. "But it will enable you to hit that backhand properly for longer."

It might also provide you with a strategic edge. In a close game, a player who's tiring rapidly is more likely to try that risky shot. A player with greater stamina will be patient and more confident—less likely to take unnecessary chances just because his or her body is saying, "enough!"

Again, running is not enough to make you a great tennis player, soccer player, or anything else. And there are other basic things you have to do to improve, including stretching and strengthening exercises and even specific kinds of "burst" running: sprints, backpedaling, side-to-side drills. But aerobic, low-intensity distance running—the kind I talk about in this book—is fundamental in any training program, especially the programs of recreational or weekend athletes—if only because it will help you enjoy your sport longer.

So here's a message to recreational sportsmen and women: For more fun, run.

QUESTION: If running is good for you, how do you explain what happened to Jim Fixx?

When the author of *The Complete Book of Running* died in 1984 of a heart attack while running in Vermont, couch potatoes and fitness naysayers nationwide had a field day. And runners, many of whom had been inspired to start by Jim Fixx's wonderful book, felt a sense of disbelief, shock, even betrayal.

Still, despite the human tragedy, Fixx's death didn't sound a death knell for the sport he helped popularize; in fact, it has continued to grow in the years since. Fixx's problem was specific, explainable, and perhaps even preventable, if the best-selling author had followed his own advice.

"One of the things he talks about in his book is the importance of listening to your own body," says Dr. Peters. Running significantly reduces the risk of heart attacks, but it does not prevent them. And one risk factor no running program can overcome is who your parents are. In Fixx's case, both his father and grandfather had died at relatively young ages of heart disease. "He inherited that tendency," says Peters, suggesting that close attention must be paid to family history—whether it's Fixx's or yours. "He had a family history that mandated more attention and concern than he apparently paid to it."

MYTH: Running will ruin your knees.

Maybe—if you run too far, too often, and without following the precautions discussed later in this book. But for most runners, it shouldn't be a problem.

An important study conducted among former collegiate cross-country runners and swimmers helped confirm this. Over 500 runners and 200 swimmers were surveyed. Their average age was 57. Among the runners, only 2 percent reported severe hip or knee pain, and 15.5 percent had moderate pain. Among the swimmers, the incidence of severe pain was slightly higher—2.4 percent; 19.5 percent had moderate pain. Keep in mind that these runners, all of whom attended college between 1930 and 1960, were training and competing in the dark ages of the sport: They ran heavy mileage with sneakers and probably without doing any of the stretching and strengthening exercises that help keep most runners on the roads today.

An impressive piece of evidence on this topic was found in a recent magazine story that cited numerous studies and concluded that exercise did not contribute to arthritis of the knees—or anywhere else, for that matter. The writer not only recommended that readers pursue an exercise program but also related how much she enjoyed running herself. A picture that ran with the article confirmed this: She looked trim, vigorous, and much younger than her 51 years. The magazine was *Arthritis Today*, and the author, Maxine Rock, has had spinal arthritis for 20 years.

MYTH: To get the benefits of running, you have to do it every day.

With the exception of elite competitors, most "real" runners generally train four to five times a week. This frequency is not only recommended but has been shown to be

17

optimal for improving performance and minimizing injuries.

MYTH: No pain, no gain.

No way. Distance running is not sprinting. It's not conducted at an out-of-breath, hell-bent-for-leather pace. When coaches and physiologists talk about the comfort zone in training, that's exactly what they mean. Most of your running should take place at an intensity level that is comfortable. This may not be true every minute of every run you do, especially when you're just starting, but once you've established your endurance base, it's going to feel fine. On some days, it will feel fabulous, which is why so many of us continue to run.

And you don't have to run hard every day. Competitive runners generally follow a hard-easy regimen: a day of hard effort alternating with one of less intense training. That keeps them from getting stale and from breaking down, which is what happens to most runners or athletes in any sport who go full tilt every day, day after day.

As far as that "no pain, no gain" line goes, it's passé in almost every form of fitness activity, especially running. We've replaced it with a new cliché, but one worth remembering: Train, don't strain.

QUESTION: If it's so much fun, how come all the runners I see are frowning?

Look again, especially when you see two or more runners training together. Chances are they'll be running along, gabbing, chatting, laughing. As you'll discover, it is fun—despite the pained looks on some solitary runners' faces.

I have a theory about that, by the way. I think it has something to do with male ego—with the gung-ho, macho attitude guys tend to have about anything physical. Watch an all-women's race—such as the nationally televised Advil Mini Marathon in Central Park—and you'll see lots of smiling faces among the participants in the middle and back of the pack. These ladies have the right idea—and the right attitude. Have fun when you run!

MYTH: Only skinny people can run well.

Although it's true that the world's best distance runners are generally small-boned and thin, bigger people can and do perform very well on the road. "People who like to run don't come in only little bodies," said 1972 Olympic gold medal marathon winner Frank Shorter, who, at 140 pounds, is lighter than the "big" women road racers who now compete in their own weight categories. The "Clydesdale" divisions—a name that is used with pride by the bigger runners—are open to women over 145 pounds and men over 200. Many of these runners are very fast and do very well in races. But what's more important is that all of them enjoy the benefits of the sport. So can you, no matter what your frame.

Also, keep in mind that weight isn't as important as body composition: that is, the percentage of fat versus lean muscle mass in your body. Do you look fat? Are your clothes fitting more tightly than they once did? Can you pinch an inch? If so, chances are you need to lose some body fat, and running may be just the way to do it.

These are the myths . . . now let's look at the facts.

2

WHAT YOU NEED
TO RUN

A friend of mine was sitting by the window of his running-apparel store one afternoon when a large, middle-aged jogger went shuffling by. The fellow was wearing a top-of-the-line Gore-Tex running suit and a pair of running shoes that looked like something out of a NASA laboratory. He had a Walkman draped over his head, a sun visor mounted on his forehead, and sports sunglasses wrapped around his face. There was a heart monitor strapped around his chest and a watch on his wrist. Around his waist he wore a fanny pack, and stuck in a holster like a six-gun was his water bottle.

Bob Cook, the store owner, waved to the fellow and then sighed. "If there were a hundred more out there like him, I could retire."

The fact of the matter is, Bob will probably have to keep working until he's 65. Why? Because runners like that fashion plate are few and far between. Most runners like thing simple, which is one of the great virtues of this sport. You don't need a boat, a racket, or a closet full of special gear to get out and run. You don't need to be mechanically inclined or technically skilled. And you certainly don't need a wrist computer, a personal stereo, or a utility belt in order to go out and do 3 miles.

I suspect that for many runners, that's part of the fun. In a world where most of us spend so much of our time dealing with computers, voice messaging systems, fax machines, and various other modern conveniences and annoyances, there's something refreshing about being able to lace up a pair of running shoes and leave it all behind, if only for a while.

And that's really all you need to be a runner—a decent pair of shoes and a willingness to put them to good use.

RUNNING SHOES

Why We Need Them

Running shoes are big business: In 1990, nearly 15 million pairs were sold in the United States alone. There's a reason for that, and it's not just because of Bo Jackson, Dan and Dave, and the other stars of the multimillion-dollar ad campaigns waged by the big shoe manufacturers. Time was, runners logged their miles in flimsy sneakers or high-tops. They ran and ran—and eventually ran into trouble as their bodies broke down from the accumulated shock and impact.

Although running is simple and beneficial, there's no question that it places stress on your feet and legs. When you run, your foot hits the ground with an impact of three to five times your body weight. And in the course of 1 mile, your foot strikes the ground over a thousand times. That's a lot of shock that needs to be absorbed, and that's what makes running shoes special.

These shoes are designed to cushion and stabilize your feet during this highly complex biomechanical process we call running. Running is actually a series of movements— or "articulations," as doctors call them—that most of us aren't even aware of as we run. To better understand why you need a special shoe, it might be helpful to understand a little more about how this process works.

"Running is a controlled falling movement," explains sports podiatrist Dr. Edward Fryman. "That is, it's like falling, except we put our foot in front of us." That's why running shoes are higher in the heel than normal shoes: to help us throw the "brake" on our fall—which we do with our heel.

The heel-to-toe motion is the difference between us distance runners and sprinters who power themselves forward for 100, 200, or 400 yards, pushing off the front of their feet. Long-distance runners can't do that. The body would break down after trying to run 5 miles on the balls of the feet. Instead, distance runners strike with the heel or midfoot. The arch of the foot rolls down as we land. Then we push off the first metatarsal—the ball of the foot—and move forward.

That's why running shoes are flexible in the middle and front. They're built to allow the foot the flexibility it needs to go through its motion. See for yourself: You can take a running shoe by the toe and bend it to a 90-degree angle. Your conservative dress blacks will never get that bent out of shape. Unlike other kinds of footgear, running shoes also provide some extra cushioning in the ball of the foot, because as we go from heel to forefoot, we tend to slap the ground.

After cushioning and flexibility comes stability—the third key element in a running shoe. Although we move in only one direction when we run, our feet tend to roll from side to side. This rotation of the foot inward and downward—so that we tend to run on the inner margins of the feet—is called pronation. Contrary to what some runners think, we all pronate; it's just a question of degree. Excessive pronation can be a problem because it can throw your knees out of alignment as you run. Fortunately, there are running shoes designed to help control this. Hard heel counters and stabilizers at the rear of the shoe can help control overpronation as well as the other common foot-motion flaw, supination, which means that the feet don't roll inward enough, and the runner tends to land too much on the outer heel.

To help us run properly and accommodate the biomechanics of the motion, running shoes have become highly sophisticated. When you go into a running-shoe store—which is where you should buy your footgear—you may be in for a shock, not only at the price tag (many models go for well over $100) but also at the diversity of models. There are shoes of all colors and styles. There are ultralight shoes for racing on the track, sturdier shoes for running on the roads, trail running shoes for those who like to run cross-country, and cross-training shoes for those who want one shoe for many sports. There are shoes with torsion bars on the outsole or bottom part of the shoes for added stability and others with nubs, ripples, waffles, and grooves of carbonized rubber to help your feet grab the road like a radial tire. Shoemakers use gels, air cushions, and plastic slabs to provide extra cushioning and, truth be told, to differentiate their shoes from those of the competition.

So where do you begin? How do you make the choice among all these different brands, features, and technologies?

How To Buy Them

To start you off in this wonderfully simple sport, I have some wonderfully simple advice when it comes to shoes. Don't worry about them just yet. And don't use the lack of a good pair of running shoes as an excuse not to get out there and get started.

Dr. Fryman, the sports podiatrist, believes that the kind of graduated walking-running program recommended for beginners can be done with any decent pair of sneakers—not the beat-up ones you keep in the garage for garden work, but a good sturdy pair. They'll be just fine for the first couple of weeks, when you're going to be doing more walking than running.

Typical running shoe: Look for a raised heel, flexible center, extra cushioning at the ball of the foot, reflectors for running at night, and—most importantly—comfort when you run. *Illustration: Christine Erikson*

THE ESSENTIAL RUNNER

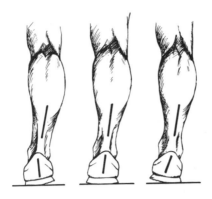

Buying The Right Shoes: Place your sneakers on a flat surface and look at them at eye level. Do they slouch? Is one or both leaning inward or outward? Minor motion control "problems" can be corrected with the right pair of shoes.

Illustration: Christine Erikson

When you're ready to run 3 miles or so, then you're ready for a trip to your local running-shoe store. Again, I recommend that you go to a specialty store, even though you can probably find good running shoes—often at a lower price—at large retail outlets. What you won't get at a department store, and what you need as a beginner, is good advice from a knowledgeable salesperson.

Experience shows that most such salespeople tend to be found in specialty running stores. Experience also shows that you don't have to part with a portrait of Benjamin Franklin to get a good pair of shoes, but you should be prepared to spend about $60 to $70. Much more than that, and you've probably bought shoes intended for someone running a lot more and a lot harder than you are at this point. Much less than that, and you could be gambling with injuries down the road.

Now, some thoughts about your shoe-shopping trip: Before you go, take a close look at the sneakers you've been walking in. Put them on a flat surface, such as a table, and get down and look at them at eye level. Do they slouch? Is one or both leaning inward or outward? If the answer is yes, you might have a motion control "problem"—and I use that word guardedly—that could be corrected with the right pair of shoes. Then look at the wear patterns on the sole: If the inner part of the sole seems more worn out than the outer, you may be an overpronator. If the outer heels have greater wear, you may be supinating. Either way, this is information the shoe salesperson needs to know. When in doubt, bring your sneakers along.

Experts recommend that you go shopping for your shoes in the afternoon, when your feet are their largest. You should wear the same or a similar pair of socks as the ones you'll be running in (more about socks in a moment).

I'm not going to tell you what you should ask the salesperson at the running-shoe store. Instead, here are five questions that the salesperson should ask *you*. And if you're not asked, then you shouldn't be buying—at least not at that store:

1. How long have you been running?

2. How much mileage are you doing?

3. Where do you do most of your running?

4. How much do you weigh?

5. Are you aware of any pronation or supination problems?

Make sure that the salesperson measures both your feet. Most of us are asymmetrical—meaning that one foot is slightly larger than the other. When that's the case, you should be fitted for the larger foot. A good salesperson should be able to tell—even if you can't—whether your feet are wider or narrower than most.

Then, you'll be shown the various models mounted on the wall or in a display case. Don't be intimidated or overly awed with all the bells and whistles. "Don't worry about the technology," says running-apparel store owner Bob Cook, himself an accomplished runner. "Worry about the fit and the comfort."

A good-fitting running shoe should be snug but not tight. There should be a little room—about half an inch—in the toe box. If you plan to run at night, you may want to get a pair with reflectors in the heels or on the sides, to allow you—or at least your shoes—to be seen in the dark. If you're a bigger person, you may want to look for a shoe that has sock liners or extra cushioning, which usually comes in the form of more ethylene vinyl acetate (EVA)—the synthetic material that is used in most insoles.

The shoes should feel comfortable when you run. Most store owners will allow you to run down the block and back, or at least around the floor of the store, to test different models. The shoes should also feel like they're giving you the support and shock absorption you expect. Whether that support comes through a compressed air or gel system doesn't really matter. What counts is how it feels on your feet.

Although I hear people carp all the time about the cost of running shoes, they're really cost-effective when you consider that a good pair can last a year. Still, you should be aware of the signs of wear-out. The key is the black rubberized material on the outsole of the shoe. If it's shredding or worn through, the shoe is not dissipating the shock as well as it should be. After a few months, you may want to put your shoes up on a flat surface again for another "tilt test."

THE WELL-DRESSED RUNNER
IN WINTER OR SUMMER

The well-dressed runner is one who's comfortable and dry. Looking stylish is a distant third. Most runners don't look so hot when they're pounding the pavement anyway. So why worry?

Staying dry is another matter. If your clothes don't properly absorb moisture, and the perspiration lays on your skin, you could get a chill, which could lead to a cold or, even worse, to hypothermia in the winter. A sweaty pair of shorts can rub against the leg or crotch, causing painful chafing. Having survived a couple of long runs where that happened to me, let me tell you, it's no fun.

Such problems can be easily avoided by choosing the right clothing to run in. Let's work our way up from the feet. Your socks should be thin, soft, and smooth. There are various kinds of running socks that have extra padding around the toes. But you can run with almost any pair of socks, provided they're a cotton blend. All-cotton socks tend to retain moisture. My test for socks: Are they soft and comfortable enough that they make you say "aaaah" as you pull them over your feet? Do you forget you have them on while you're running? If the answer to both is yes, that's a good pair of socks to run in.

Mesh nylon shorts are ideal. They're soft, lightweight, and throw the moisture off as opposed to those old grey sweatshorts you wore in gym class, which held water like a sponge.

To top it off, a soft, comfortable T-shirt will do. Be careful of stiff, new shirts, which may chafe your nipples. In hot weather, you may want to consider a sleeveless tank top or, better yet, a mesh singlet. Remember, when it's hot, you want as much of your skin exposed as possible so the sweat can dry. Every summer, I wince as I see people running around in heavy sweatsuits even on the hottest days. They think they're burning more fat, but they're actually just losing water weight—which is replaced as soon as they step up to a water fountain. It can also be dangerous. When in doubt, underdress.

How about winter running? Well, your running-store salesperson will be happy to show you cold-weather running suits. He or she will be even happier if you buy one, since they're very expensive. No question about it: Synthetic fabrics and blends such as Lycra, Thermax, and Gore-Tex have revolutionized outdoor sports apparel. They're light, comfortable, and will keep you snug and dry in even the most inclement weather. But that doesn't mean they're essential. "You don't have to invest hundreds of dollars to stay warm and dry in the winter," says store owner Cook.

Basically, you need clothing that breathes properly and "wicks"—or draws—the moisture away from your body. And don't forget what your mom told you about dressing in layers: A T-shirt, turtleneck sweater, and windbreaker will get you through most damp, cold, windy days. If you want to be warm, dry, *and* look snazzy, you can invest $40 or so in a polypropylene top, a nylon shell (about $35) to go over it, and a matching pair of polypropylene pants (about $40). (But remember, you're likely to need long pants only in really cold weather. Your legs tend to stay warm when running simply because they're moving.)

The most important articles of winter running apparel are probably the smallest: a hat and gloves—the real keys to beating the cold. "A hat and gloves will keep you out longer than someone in a Gore-Tex suit bareheaded," says Cook. The best hat is probably a knit or wool ski cap. And unless you're planning to run along the Bering Strait in winter, that's probably all you'll need. If you do live in especially cold climes, however, you may want to consider a balaclava—which wraps around your head and chin commando-style—or even one of the various knit masks that allow you to breathe while covering most of your face. Your gloves should be soft and comfortable too. In fact, many runners prefer mittens to gloves because you can curl your fingers up inside.

The only area we've overlooked is underwear. It's a bit indelicate to discuss, perhaps, which is why it hardly ever is. But you can't dispute its importance to comfortable running. Most of the good mesh running shorts mentioned earlier have elastic waistbands and crepe liners, built-in briefs, or so-called comfort panels to keep you running easily. But in the winter, you may not want to wear a pair of running shorts under a pair of pants. Athletic supporters are very uncomfortable when you're running. My recommendations: a pair of snug-fitting briefs.

Women may want to consider the specially designed jogging or sports bras, which are carried in most lingerie departments or at running specialty stores. Here, I defer to Henley Gibble and Ellen Wessel of the Road Runner's Club of America, who offer this advice in a pamphlet on women's running: "Wearing a comfortable bra can prevent the irritation on sensitive nipples from tee shirt fabrics. A bra to run in should have smooth seams and should cover or eliminate hooks and clips.... Fuller busted women might be more comfortable in a molded cup and sturdier construction. The newer fabrics now available in bras are comfortable during movement yet eliminate bounces. Ideally the straps should come together at the back to keep them from falling off the shoulders."

ACCESSORIES

Reflective Clothing

Reflective vests cost only about $10 to $15, but they could save your life. These lightweight nylon vests have reflective strips sewn onto them, which make you look like a bouncing stick figure to motorists in the dark. You can also buy reflective wristbands, neon shoelaces, and even 1-inch strips of reflective material that you can stick to your clothing. Reflective white T-shirts are a new addition to this category and, as mentioned earlier, many shoes have reflectors. Any or all of them are worthwhile investments if you plan to do your training at dusk or at night.

Hats and Sunscreen

With the increasing awareness of skin cancer, it makes sense to apply a sunscreen before you run and to wear a hat. On hot, sunny days, however, when a hat would trap the heat dissipated through the head, you may want to try one of those lightweight wraparound visors that shield your eyes and face from the sun.

Petroleum Jelly

One of the most useful products to everyday runners is a jar of petroleum jelly. In marathons, they have big glops of the stuff, there for the taking, at water stops. The reason? Running chafes—particularly when you run longer distances. To help minimize the risk of that painful rubbing of skin against skin, or against fabric, many runners apply petroleum jelly to the nipples, crotch, and toes before a race or a long run.

Personal Stereos

It's nice to run to the sound of music, but runners lost in a pop song or a symphony can't hear cars, dogs, or other people coming up on them. If you're on a track or a treadmill, you can get away with it sometimes, but my recommendations is not to get started. If you want music to run by, listen to your "psych-up" tunes while you're stretching at home; cue these records up on your mental turntable and play them in your head while you run.

Key Holders

This may be the most frequently asked "dumb" question I hear from beginners: "I know this is a dumb question, but what do you do with your keys when you run?" Actually, it's not a stupid question at all. Trying to figure out what to do with my keys used to drive me crazy when I first started running. So what do you do? Well, many running shorts come with a key pocket where you can stash your home or car key and maybe even a $10 bill, just in case. You can also buy a Velcro wristband to carry keys, money, and ID (a good thing to take with you, especially if you're running the roads), for about $5. Or you can do what I do: Simply fasten your key to the inside of your shorts or pants with a safety pin.

Fanny Packs

If you've got a lot of stuff you want to carry—like a plastic water bottle—you may want to consider one of these zippered pouches attached to a belt that you wrap around your waist. The important thing here is to get one that you can tighten enough so that there's no slipping and sliding as you run. Depending on their size and the amount of insulation they offer—there are even some that you can carry hot fluids in—the packs cost from about $15 to $35.

Sports Watches

If there's anything a runner needs other than shoes, socks, shorts, and shirt, it's a way to keep track of duration and speed. Sweep-second hand watches won't do the trick. You need a digital watch, preferably one with a stopwatch function, allowing you to gauge exactly how long it took to finish a mile or two or three.

There are lots of other features on good sports watches, some of which few runners use or even fully understand. You can spend a lot of money and get a watch that tells you everything from military time to the temperature. Or you can spend $35 or so for a watch that has the stopwatch feature and an adjustable wristband and is water-resistant. Other than that, it should tell time, which means that you can wear it even when you're not running.

Heart Monitors

Heart monitors keep track of your heart rate while you exercise. The electrical activity of the heart is "watched" by conductive rubber electrodes built into an elastic strap worn around the chest. When the heart contracts, the electrodes send the signal along to a transmitter in the strap, which passes a corresponding radio signal to the receiver, located in a special wristwatch. If your heart rate goes under or over your preset limit—your so-called target heart rate—the watch beeps.

As the president of one of the largest manufacturers of heart monitors explained it to me, the purpose is similar to that of the speedometer in your car, which helps you get from point A to point B without getting a ticket. The heart monitor tells you when you've exceeded your cardiovascular speed limit.

There's one problem with that logic. There are signs on the road that tell us not to exceed speed limits of 30 or 55 mph but your personal cardiovascular speed limit is not as easily determined. That shouldn't be construed as a knock against heart monitors. Some of the top endurance athletes in the world use them, and they can be very useful to the average runner or cyclist too. If you have a history of heart problems, your cardiologist will probably tell you that you must wear one. But if you're just starting out and healthy, a heart monitor may not be essential.

"Taking your pulse constantly can drive you nuts," says cardiologist Peters. "It takes the fun out of exercise. And a heart monitor can be intimidating, especially if you try to set it yourself." His recommendations: If you decide to invest in a heart monitor—the least expensive models start at about $125—consult your doctor. He or she can help you set your own predetermined cardiovascular "speed limits." Peters believes, and I agree, that technology and money—or the lack thereof—shouldn't be barriers to starting a running or exercise program.

3

GETTING STARTED

Whenever people ask me about starting a running program, I tell them: "Take a hike." That may sound like a glib response, but it's the truth. A good running program starts by putting one foot in front of the other—slowly. It's not a sport to be hurried into. "People seem to think running is much easier than it is," says Dr. Peters, the cardiologist. "So I tell them it's harder than they think it is, and it'll take longer than they want it to take."

That's not meant to be discouraging. It's simply a warning against trying to go too far, too fast. "If you're in reasonably good shape, you could probably go out today and run for 45 minutes," says Dr. Fryman, the sports podiatrist. "But you'd wake up so sore you'd never want to do it again."

Instead, you should begin by going out for a brisk walk. Don't worry about speed or distance, or about how far your neighbor or son-in-law runs. Just walk as far as you can go—comfortably—for 20 to 30 minutes, four times a week, for about two weeks. Use that time to read ahead in this book, and learn more about the sport you're about to enter.

Remember, walking is a beneficial exercise in and of itself. Proponents of walking have become quite strident (pardon the pun) in its defense; some say that it's even better for you than running. That's arguable—but not worth arguing. You can enjoy both—as I do—although I think you'll find that running is more challenging and more of a workout. The point is, don't think you're wasting your time by walking before you run. You're not: You're burning calories and improving your fitness—just not as quickly as you will when you actually start running.

That should come after a couple of weeks, when you can walk briskly, nonstop, for 45 minutes. But don't expect—or even try—to do a mile the first time. The transition from walker to runner is one that takes place step by step—and I mean that figuratively as well as literally. When you start running, you shouldn't go too fast or for too long. The whole point of this gradual buildup is to let your body—muscles, lungs, cardiovascular system—adapt to the new but ultimately beneficial stresses you're placing on it.

For example, as I mentioned in the first chapter, you're using only about 40 percent of your lung volume as you read this. You're not going to get the other 60 percent into action just by taking one deep breath. "Be patient, be consistent, and build slowly," says Fryman. That's sound advice. Overeager novices who do too much too soon usually end up hurt, then disgusted. Soon enough, they make their way back into the easy chair, never to rise again.

Add running to your walking regimen gradually. If you're on an outdoor track—which is where you should start—walk a lap, then jog a lap. But don't try to do that for 30 minutes the first time. Maybe you can walk eight laps, jog two, walk eight, jog two. Or, if you prefer, walk for 20 minutes and jog for 10. Let your body be your guide on this, and when in doubt, slow down and walk—not a stroll, mind you, but a brisk walk.

Many coaches and top runners now talk in terms of minutes, not miles. It used to be that runners counted every mile and got so obsessive about it that they felt that anything less than 5 miles in one session or 50 in one week wasn't enough. To avoid falling into that mileage trap, you should start out thinking in terms of minutes. Don't get hung up on distance alone. Focus on the quality of your running as well as the quantity.

I know this program seems awfully conservative; it may also sound like running is an unending regimen of pain. But nothing could be further from the truth. The toughest part of running is getting started. Unless you get to the point where you're competing seriously, most of the pain and discomfort occurs in the first month, during the adaptation process. This is why an estimated 90 percent of those who quit running do so in the first four weeks.

I don't want you to become a statistic, so please be patient. The more conservative you are, the less discomfort you'll feel as you make the transition from walker to runner.

WHERE TO RUN

Let's face it: Many folks just starting out, particularly those who are a bit overweight, are self-conscious. They don't want to be seen in shorts and T-shirts by their neighbors. They don't want to be seen walking back home after they started out running, as if they have failed in the pursuit of fitness. It's silly, but it's human nature.

On the track, no one puts on any airs. Even serious runners walk or jog laps between their fast intervals. It's safe (no cars), it's precise (a quarter mile or 400 meters), and it's an environment conducive to getting in shape. You'll meet like-minded people there; no one is going to look and stare at you or make comments about running, about Jim Fixx, or about how long so-and-so's grandfather lived even though he smoked a pack of cigarettes a day.

Of course, if you prefer, or if there's no track accessible to you, you can just walk out your door—which is another reason that running is such a wonderfully simple sport. If you want to start out running the roads, choose a scenic "loop" course through your neighborhood without too much traffic or too many turns. You may want to measure it using your car odometer (precise enough for our purposes). Then, instead of adding a half or full lap on the track, you can try to increase your distance by a telephone pole, or a block, or a half-minute as you make the walking-to-running transition.

Many communities have lots of wonderful trails and paths to run on, in parks or preserves, many of them well-measured and marked. I urge you to discover and explore the ones in your area. But don't choose a course that requires a drive of more than 5 or 10 minutes from your home or workplace. Where you run can often determine whether you run. The idea is to make it part of your regular daily routine. The extra 20 minutes you have to drive in order to get to an out-of-the-way running path could be one more excuse for not going at all. And the last thing we need is another excuse to avoid exercise!

A third option is a motorized treadmill. If you have access to one, great. Most health clubs now have rows of them, and they're certainly an attractive alternative on inclement days. They're also good in terms of giving you a fairly precise sense of how far and how fast you're going. You can slow them down and speed them up as you walk or run your way into shape. And when you get serious, you can even raise the incline of a treadmill to simulate hill training.

But treadmills have their drawbacks as well. First, running on them can be exceedingly dull. Some people try to deal with this by setting up a TV set in front of the treadmill so they can watch as they run. The other major problem is that using a treadmill is going to cost you money: At the very least, you'll have to pay the membership costs of a health club. And if you want one for your home, you'll have to pay at least $2,000 for a decent one. I recommend that you hold off on buying a treadmill until you're committed to your running program. Otherwise, you may be stuck with a very expensive dust collector in your basement.

One last point about where to run: Some people draw a distinction between soft and hard surfaces. It is a consideration. For example, if you're running the roads, it's preferable to run on asphalt macadam, which is a little softer than a hard concrete sidewalk. However, Fryman notes that most running injuries are the result of biomechanical problems—not the surface you run on. If finding the right surface for your runs becomes an obstacle to your running program, it's defeating the purpose. There are lots of places to run—some of them just outside your door. Why not start there?

WHEN TO RUN AND
WHO TO RUN WITH

Question: When is the best time of day to run?
Answer: Whenever it's most convenient for you.

Although we can all be classified by our "chrono-type," studies have shown that there's no significant performance advantage in exercising morning, noon, or night. However, there are definite psychological pros and cons. It's a great feeling to begin your morning with a run, but getting out of bed is tough. Lunchtime runs break up the day and give you an energy boost for the afternoon, but if you have an hour or less for lunch, you may not have enough time to change, warm up, walk or run, cool down, and shower. Although evening runs are a nice way to dissipate the tensions and frustrations of the workday, the temptations of couch and refrigerator may be too much. You may stop off at home with the intention of changing into your running clothes and never leave the house.

The key, then, is to make time for your running. Some people say that they "just can't run" in the morning. But if the morning is the only time they have, then what? I urge you to keep an open mind and be willing to get up a little earlier or have dinner a little later, if necessary. The important thing is to find a time of day or night that's going to be convenient for you, at least four times a week. You should be able to find time Saturday and Sunday, so you may only have two days a week where you have to make the time to run. Surely your health and the success of your program are worth that much.

It's also important to find someone you can run with. Most runners, myself included, believed all that "loneliness of the long-distance runner" stuff when we started. The truth is that distance running is a very social activity, and having someone with you when you start can be a big motivational boost. Committing to doing something with a friend increases the likelihood that you'll do it. "That's how I started running," said Gordon Bakoulis, a writer and nation-class female marathoner. "I would promise to meet a friend at 6:30 A.M. There were many mornings that if I hadn't known she was waiting out there in the freezing cold, I would've slept in."

PROPER FORM

To some, making the transition from walking to running is reminiscent of an earlier experiment in motion. "It's like the first time you rode a bicycle as a kid," says Larry Davidson, a running coach and consultant to the American Heart Association. "Your dad put you on your bike, gave you a push, and said, 'Start pedaling!'" Fortunately, you're not as likely to fall flat on your face when you start to run. But you may feel equally awkward—as if you're fighting your body. Davidson's recommendation: "Try not to be self-conscious about it. Just let your body take over."

True enough—but you may want to remind your body of a few facts before you do. First, running is not sprinting; distance running is a heel-toe motion. You should be landing on the midfoot or the heel when you strike the ground, and pushing off with the front of your foot. This minimizes the stress on the calves and produces a cushioning effect that helps reduce the risk of injury. It's also the most efficient foot-strike for most distance runners. And when you're asking each foot to take a thousand foot-strikes per mile, the more efficiently they can do it the better.

Second, running is not jumping. I'm often amazed when I see runners who bounce into the air with each stride. That may be good form for a triple jumper, but not for a distance runner. Your feet shouldn't be spending a great deal of time in the air. If anything, you want to shuffle, not bound your way through your run.

Finally, how you carry your upper body is almost as important as how you land and strike. What's impressive about watching elite runners is that most of them seem so relaxed and comfortable in their motion and in the way they carry themselves as they run. They're not all tensed up, and they're not flailing their arms. They're running smoothly, efficiently.

Running that way takes practice, even for gifted athletes. One high school coach in Massachusetts has his runners hold potato chips while working out: The goal is to finish the run without breaking the chip. The idea behind it is too keep the runners from tensing up from the waist up.

You don't have to run around holding snack food to improve your form, but you'd do well to keep these tips in mind:

❦ Don't tense up your shoulders.

❦ Don't ball your hands up into fists.

❦ Keep your arms bent slightly, but don't exaggerate your arm motion as if you're a miler racing toward the finish line.

The advice about relaxing your body as you run applies from head to toe. A series of local New York runs staged by disciples of the Indian guru Sri Chinmoy is called "Runners Are Smilers." How appropriate—yet how often do you see runners on the road with their faces screwed into masks of pain, determination, or effort? I'm not saying that you should run like a grinning fool, but don't tense your jaw up as if you're about to hit the beach on D day, either.

A good way to remember some of these key points about good running form is through a little rhyme that many beginner runners, myself included, recite to themselves like a running mantra: "Hands down, shoulders back, hips forward, stay relaxed." To elaborate: The hands should be held in a line close to the bottom of your running shorts, which means that you should keep your arms loose and slightly bent. Shoulders back really means shoulders down, not tensed up. Hips are forward because that's the direction you're going. One study found that competitive runners who tended to lean forward were more efficient and therefore ran faster. I also find that it takes a little stress off the lower back. Above all, stay relaxed as you run. If you do, you'll find that good form will follow function.

HILL RUNNING

Sooner or later, you're going to run into hills.

Eamonn Coghlan swore at them while he was training for the Olympics. Now he swears by them. "Phenomenal way to build strength!" says Coghlan, the world indoor record holder for the mile (3 minutes, 49.78 seconds).

"Running hills breaks up your rhythm and forces your muscles to adapt to new stresses. The result? You're stronger."

Another Olympian, Jeff Galloway, agrees. "Hill training is the single best way to develop leg strength," says Galloway. "And once you learn proper form, it doesn't have to hurt."

The great secret to hill running, he says, is quick foot turnover and a shortened stride length. In other words, instead of pushing up the hill, scurry up it with shorter, quicker strides. Plant your foot directly under your body, keep your chest up and out, and swing your arms rhythmically.

Going downhill, Galloway recommends that you lean slightly forward and let gravity do the work. However, stay in control and don't let your stride length increase too much. That could give your knees a real pounding.

BREATHING

People who have been breathing successfully for years get very concerned about it when they start running. Some think they should keep their mouths closed in order to filter the air through the nose. Others try to keep a certain rhythm. Still others, particularly beginners, tend to take short, rapid gasps.

We normally breathe through the chest by contracting the muscles of the rib cage, shoulder region, and diaphragm—the muscles that separate the chest from the abdominal cavity. But chest breathing is not necessarily the most efficient way to breathe while running. In fact, says Bryant A. Stamford, director of the Health Promotion Wellness Center at the University of Louisville, chest

Correct Running Form: Push off from the front of foot and land on heel. Feet should not spend a long time in the air; rather, they should move as in a shuffle. Relax—do not tense shoulders or ball up hands into fists. Keep arms bent slightly but do not exaggerate arm motion.

breathing while you run may cause discomfort among beginners. "That's one reason why a novice jogger hates it," Stamford was quoted as saying in an Associated Press story. "The breathing is so terribly unnatural that it sends signals to the person, 'I don't like this.'"

Because chest breathing does not eliminate as much carbon dioxide, the higher level of this waste gas triggers your body to breathe faster, according to Stamford. Belly breathing, which utilizes the abdominal muscles as well as the diaphragm, pushes out more carbon dioxide. So, in theory, it's more efficient and should help you feel more comfortable while you run.

Does that mean that you should practice belly breathing before you run? No, although you might want to be aware of it when you start. As Stamford points out, the body will always find the most efficient way to get things done. And for most people, the most efficient way to get as much oxygen in and as much carbon dioxide out while running is through belly breathing.

The good news about this is that your body will switch over to belly breathing naturally, as it feels the need to. So sleepless nights over how you breathe are not necessary. Eventually your breathing will evolve into a pattern that's efficient for you. In fact, you won't even know you're doing it.

STARTING AND FINISHING

Some people seem to think that a proper warm-up means doing sit-ups and push-ups or touching their toes a few times. Not so. The purpose of the warm-up is to elevate your heart rate gradually. So whatever you do should be easy and sustained. If you're at the point in your program where most of your workout is fast walking, start with moderately paced walking for 5 to 10 minutes (again, using your body as your guide). If you're already running, start with a fast walk or a slow jog. Stretching is important, but it's not necessarily the best warm-up, as discussed in the next chapter.

Misconceptions also exist about what a cool-down is or when it should begin. Most runners pick up speed at the end of their run to make their last lap or mile the fastest. That's a mistake. "The heroic sprint to the finish is one of the worst misconceptions," says Jeff Galloway, the noted running coach, author, and former Olympian. "It's more likely to produce an injury than anything else. The time to accelerate is the middle of the workout." The last 5 or 10 minutes of your run, Galloway maintains, should be done at a slower pace, followed by 10 minutes of walking.

The biggest mistake you can make after a hard run is to fling yourself to the ground for a rest—or jump in your car and drive home. When you stop suddenly after a hard effort, your heart is beating vigorously, but the blood has pooled in your legs, leaving less available for the heart and brain. This is why some people feel dizzy after a hard workout—or sore the next day. "We want to keep the blood flowing back where it's needed," says Dr. Bob Otto, director of the Human Performance Lab at Adelphi University in New York, "to flush out the lactate acid and other metabolic waste products that build up in the muscle fibers during the workout."

This leads us to the golden rule of cool: Keep moving. That's how you start, and that's how you should finish your workout. Try to visualize it as a gently sloped plateau: gradually building up your intensity level, then running at a comfortable but challenging pace, then gradually scaling it down again.

HOW HARD?

I used to work out at a health club in mid-Manhattan that catered to older male executives. These men—many of whom were overweight and had heart problems—were taught the importance of monitoring their heart rates. They were warned about what could happen to them if they exceeded those rates and were urged to take their pulses before, during, and after their workouts.

And so, as you walked around the floor of this club, you'd see people spending less time on the treadmills and stationary bikes and more time staring up at the clock with their fingers on their necks, nervously counting seconds and computing their heart rates. They seemed to be more worried about their pulses than their progress, and they definitely did not seem to be enjoying themselves.

I'm not trying to discount the importance of being aware of your heart rate, especially for those high-risk individuals. I said it before in the discussion of heart monitors and I'll say it again: If you have a history of heart problems, or if you are an individual at risk—a determination your physician will help you make when you get your prerunning checkup—you must keep track of your heart rate to make sure you're working hard enough, but not too hard.

The formula that's still most widely used is 220 minus your age; 60 to 70 percent of that is considered your target heart rate, the rate at which your heart should be beating while you exercise. For example, the target heart rate of a

Workout Intensity Curve

35-year old man would be 220–35 = 180. Seventy percent of 180 is 126. You can take your pulse on the thumb-side of your wrist or at the carotid artery in your neck. Count the number of beats in 15 seconds and multiply by four.

However, many cardiologists, exercise physiologists, coaches, and trainers now use an easier way to gauge the intensity level for individuals who are healthy and have no background of heart problems. It's called the "talk test," and it simply means that if you can carry on a conversation while you're running, you're working at the right intensity level. If you can't—if you're huffing and puffing—you need to slow down; you're going too hard. If you can not only talk but sing (no matter how off-key), you're probably not working hard enough. Although the talk test is a good way to determine how hard you're working your body, coach Davidson believes that some of it is in your head as well: "I think there's a direct relationship between what you're thinking and what you're feeling," he says. "If you can have a coherent thought process going on while you run, you're okay. When you push too hard, all you can think about is the pain."

HOW LONG?

Ask veterans to pinpoint the moment they felt they had "become" runners, and they'll likely gaze off into space with a puzzled look. The transition takes place so gradually that, after awhile, you begin to forget there was a time when you couldn't run.

But beginners will savor that magic moment. And it will come, believe me. After about 4 to 6 weeks, depending on your age and exercise history, you should be able to comfortably walk and run for 45 minutes (25 running, 20 walking). From there it's just a matter of reducing the amount of walking time and increasing the time spent running. Follow the sample schedules in the appendix of this book, which will lead you up to 3 miles, 5 miles, and even a 10-kilometer (6.2-mile) run. That may sound like a long way when you're just starting, but the stronger you get, the shorter those distances will seem. Then you're golden. "Once you hit your stride," says Dr. Peters, "you'll find it gets easier and easier."

Once you've reached the point where you're running, as opposed to walking, 20 to 30 minutes four or five times a week—or about 15 miles a week—a small celebration is in order. "Give yourself a pat on the back," says Davidson. "You've reached an important milestone. You've now equaled [Dr. Ken] Cooper's recommendations for cardiovascular fitness."

This, some feel, is all you need. However, most cardiologists today believe that 20 minutes—long considered the standard minimum duration of any cardiovascular fitness activity—may not be sufficient. The key is to find an intensity level that will allow you to comfortably exercise nonstop for 45 minutes. "You've got to get past that 20-minute mark to get the real benefits of aerobic exercise," says Peters. "After 20 minutes, your body is telling you to stop. But if you keep going you'll feel reenergized."

What happens is that after 20 minutes, the average body runs out of sugar—its short-term source of energy—and must switch over to its secondary energy stores: triglycerides, fat, complex carbohydrates, and cholesterol—precisely the things you want your body to burn. For this reason, 45 minutes is probably a better target if your goal is weight loss or weight control. That 45 minutes can be spent running and walking.

Eventually, of course, you'll get to the point where you can run continuously for that amount of time. Sooner than that, however, you'll come to a point where you'll feel you've made the transition. It's hard to say when that will be, because it varies from person to person, and it's as much in the mind as it is in the body. But rest assured, it will come. One day you'll go out and run comfortably, naturally, without worrying about your form or your pulse rate. You'll feel great. You'll feel like you've been doing this all along.

Congratulations. You're a runner.

RUNNING, FITNESS, AND INJURY PREVENTION

Ask yourself why you wanted to start a running program. If you're like most of us, it's probably because you wanted to lose weight, get in shape, or improve your fitness. Which begs the question: Just what is fitness, anyway? A state of mind, a pair of chiseled biceps, a hook for selling cross-training shoes? The fact is, you could run a two-day seminar trying to come up with a definition acceptable to everybody. We don't have the time or space for that here, so let's try to find a definition that's useful for you.

Joseph Rottino, a retired English teacher and marathon runner who lost 30 pounds in his pursuit of fitness, offers this definition: Fitness allows you to meet the daily demands of life without putting your body under any undue physiological or psychological stress.

Dr. Ralph Paffenbarger of Stanford University, author of a landmark study that linked exercise with greater longevity and reduced coronary heart disease, says "The definition of [fitness] isn't a simple one." Longer life and healthier hearts are obviously a part of fitness—and of running. But, as Paffenbarger explains, there are athletic characteristics of fitness such as speed, strength, power, agility, balance, reaction time, and coordination as well as health characteristics such as blood pressure, cholesterol levels, and body composition—the percent of body fat versus muscle tissue. An individual's metabolism is also part of what determines fitness. As Paffenbarger explains, these are things we can't control but can influence. You can't lower your blood pressure by closing your eyes and wishing for it; nor, in all probability, can you remake yourself into a Cher or Carl Lewis clone, even by working out every day for the rest of your life. However, you can make big improvements; you can be the best you can be by following sound exercise and nutrition programs, as you are starting to do now.

In that sense, Paffenbarger contends that a large part of physical fitness is in the mind. "General attitudes influence our health and our risk of avoiding certain chronic diseases," he says. "Proper attitude becomes increasingly important with the process of aging . . . thinking that you can do something about your health. It's not God's will. It's not chance. It's a proper attitude."

As we've discussed, running seems to promote a healthier attitude. But running alone does not achieve total fitness—which is why I've taken some time here to try to define it. "Running does give you cardiovascular protection," says Dr. Tom Scandalis of the New York College of Osteopathic Medicine. "But it's not going to help you lift a heavy bag of groceries or mend a fence. So if you're looking to improve your overall fitness, you'll need to do more than run."

This is why we now need to move ahead from our working definitions of fitness and develop a "working-out" definition of fitness—one you can use to help build or refine your exercise program; one in which running will play a primary role.

THE FITNESS PYRAMID

Lists of the athletic characteristics of fitness, such as the one offered by Dr. Paffenbarger, tend to sound like job descriptions for a Michael Jordan stand-in. Few of us have the genes or the means to develop all those qualities. However, many exercise physiologists talk in terms of three major components of fitness:

1. *Flexibility*: We try to develop suppleness of movement and range of motion by including gentle gradual stretches either before or after our workouts. Most runners hate doing it, but all of them should.

2. *Musculoskeletal strength*: Often overlooked by runners until recently, strength is the ability to exert force against resistance. Strength training increases muscle mass and bone density and helps prevent injuries—not to mention keeping us from looking like skinny little geeks. The other benefit of strength training—muscular endurance—enables our muscles to function effectively over longer periods of time, such as during a distance run.

3. *Cardiovascular endurance*: This is the ability of your heart and lungs to use oxygen efficiently while exercising. Your running will certainly help you achieve this, but there are other forms of cardiovascular training (cross-training) that you can and should do as well.

That's the pyramid: If you're running to get fit, and if you want to be a better runner, you should make exercises that promote all three parts of your program. It's not as tough as it sounds, and it will do more than make you a better runner: It will make you fit—by definition.

FLEXIBILITY

One of the more interesting new trends in health clubs is the emergence of so-called flexibility fitness classes. An alternative to typical step aerobics or dance classes, these sessions use traditional stretches, yoga positions, and even ballet and dance movements to help participants ease muscle tension, increase range of motion, and improve posture. The instructors in these classes tell me that most of their students come from two populations: runners and former high-impact aerobic dancers. All of these people have joints that have endured a lot of pounding over the years, on the roads or on the hardwood floors of exercise studios. None of them seemed to give stretching much thought in the past. Now, as their knees crack and their backs ache, they're paying the price.

For years, runners pooh-poohed stretching. Who wanted to stand around trying to touch their toes when the road beckoned? How could a hamstring stretch compare with the feeling of a good hard 5-mile run? The truth is, it can't—at least, not in my book. But that doesn't mean that it shouldn't be done and that it won't make you feel good. It will—even if it seems too passive, not as strenuous or as invigorating as walking, running, or lifting weights. I recommend that you check your local Y, health club, or adult education program to see if they have a flexibility or yoga class. If they do, I urge you to fit it into your schedule and make it part of your running program. It will make that program more successful by making you more flexible and less prone to the kind of overuse injuries that plagued a generation of running-boomers who overlooked this important part of the fitness pyramid. Flexibility is also a key factor in performance: Flexible, stretched muscles are capable of contracting more forcefully, enabling you to generate more force and run faster.

Of course, you can improve your flexibility without taking a class by following a regular stretching program of your own. Stretching guru and author Bob Anderson says that the first goal in stretching should be to reduce muscle tension and that the first decision to be made about a stretching program is not what, but when. The "when" of stretching has been the cause of much debate in physiology circles. Traditionally, stretching was done as part of the warm-up, before you began running. But more and more experts say that the best time is after a workout, when the muscles are warm.

Anderson neatly sidesteps the argument, saying that the ideal flexibility program includes stretching both before and after the workout. What's important, he says, is not what time you stretch but simply that you stretch. It doesn't have to be when you run. Sometimes when I'm watching TV at night, I find myself sliding off the easy chair and onto the rug to do some stretches. Others like to do them whey they get out of bed in the morning.

Whenever you do them, it's important that you stretch the right way. I'm still surprised when I see runners—mostly older men—who start bouncing up and down, doing those old "cherry picker" exercises and deep knee bends. They look like extras in a World War II training film, with lines and lines of guys in white T-shirts, jumping up and down in boot-camp unison. Although calisthenics—rhythmic, freehand exercises—have their value, they are not stretching or flexibility exercises, no matter what your gym teacher told you.

The proper way to stretch isn't hard, fast, or violently. It's gradually, slowly, and *never* to the point of pain. When you stretch into a position, you should feel what Anderson calls "a mild tension." Go no further than that; hold the stretch there, and feel your muscle fibers elongate. Breathe slowly, relax, and hold it for 5 to 15 seconds. At that point, you should feel a little slackening in the muscles. If you don't, back off. Pain indicates that the body is fighting the stretch by contracting the muscles you're trying to elongate. After holding that first stretch, Anderson suggests that you stop and repeat for 10 to 20 seconds. This so-called developmental stretch will increase your flexibility.

Remember: This is not a race or a contest. Don't worry about how far you can stretch or how long you can hold it. Don't bounce when you stretch. Follow proper form— lots of people do stretches the wrong way and end up getting hurt. One way to help yourself is by being aware of the muscle groups you're working on and feeling the stretch in that area as you do each exercise.

Four for Flexibility

A good stretching regimen should emphasize all the major muscle groups. Some folks stretch instinctively, like cats, and there are lots of stretches you can do that way. But the basics might include these four:

Hamstring Stretch: Sit down and extend both legs. While keeping one leg bent at the knee, gently reach out as far as you can over extended leg. Do not try to grab toes. Repeat with other leg.

1. The hamstring stretch: This works the large muscles in the back of the thigh. It's a safer variation of the so-called hurdler's stretch. Simply sit down and extend both legs. While keeping one leg bent at the knee, gently reach out over the other extended leg as far as you can. Hold that position for up to 20 seconds, then repeat with the other leg. Don't strain yourself trying to grasp your toes; I almost pulled out my back trying to do this in a yoga class once, determined to reach my foot, as if that proved something. All it proved was that the ratio of my leg length to my trunk was greater than that of most of the others in my class. Now I simply reach as far as I can and get the benefits of the stretch without worrying if I'm going far enough.

2. The quadriceps stretch: This stretch works the large muscles in the front of the thigh, and is often done improperly. With your extended right arm against a wall for support, gently pull your right foot toward your backside with your left arm. Try to keep your knee pointing straight

Quadriceps Stretch: Extend right arm against a wall for support and gently pull your right foot towards your backside with your left arm; keep knee pointing straight to the ground. Repeat with left foot and right arm.

THE ESSENTIAL RUNNER

to the ground. (If you do this in front of a mirror, it should almost look as if an artist airbrushed out your lower leg.) Don't bend over as you do this stretch. Repeat the stretch a second time, pulling your knee back just a little further (so you can't see it when you look down). This will help increase your hip extension, giving you an even more complete stretch of the quadriceps. Repeat with the other leg.

3. The calf stretch: This helps stretch out the calf muscles and the Achilles tendon, which is important in the push-off phase of the running motion. The movement is similar to the position you might take if you were helping a motorist push his car out of a rut or a snowdrift. With both hands extended against a supporting structure, press your back heel to the ground and bend forward with your front knee. By keeping your back leg straight, you'll feel the stretch in the gastrocnemius—the upper part of the calf. Repeat with your back knee bent slightly, and you'll stretch out the soleus—the lower part of the calf—and the Achilles. Repeat with the other leg.

4. The Williams lower back stretch: One of the exercises commonly prescribed for people with lower back problems, this stretch also prevents the same and stretches out the hamstrings and hips. Lie on your back with both legs extended. Lift your left leg, reach under it with your arms, and bring it slowly toward the chest. Repeat with the opposite leg.

MUSCULAR STRENGTH
AND ENDURANCE

Eamonn Coghlan, world record holder for the indoor mile, remembers the time his coach at Villanova, the leg-

Calf Stretch: With both hands extended against a supporting wall, press your back heel to the ground and bend forward with your front knee, keeping the back leg straight.

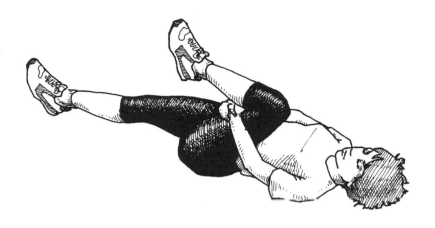

Williams Lower Back Stretch: Lie on your back with both legs extended. Lift your left leg, reach under it with your arms, as if hugging it, and slowly bring it toward your chest.

endary Jumbo Elliot, spotted some distance runners doing leg extensions on one of the then-newfangled weight training machines. "'Goddamn it!' Jumbo said," recalls Coghlan with a laugh, "'The best goddam way to get stronger for running is to goddam run.'"

Such has been the dominant philosophy of coaches and competitive runners since the dawn of the sport. But the thinking has now changed. Although everyone agrees that the most important part of training for running is running, evidence has mounted that supplemental strength exercises can enhance performance and prevent injury.

Although running builds aerobic fitness, it doesn't do much for your total body strength. In fact, a recent 10-year study of distance runners found that many had actually lost muscle mass in their upper bodies. This has implications beyond your appearance in a T-shirt. Stronger muscles enable you to hold form longer during a run, which can prevent injuries. As you tire and your running form begins to deteriorate, you begin to lean forward, which strains your back and can, in turn, strain your gluteal and hamstring muscles, leading to injuries. With a strong body, however, you can maintain proper posture and avoid such problems.

In general, strong muscles, tendons, and ligaments are less likely to tear or rupture. Well-conditioned muscles absorb shock better and work better to balance your body as you run. I'm not talking about bodybuilder-type muscles. Many runners, particularly women, fear that strength training of any kind will build too much bulk. This is a myth. Most of us couldn't look like Mr. or Ms. America— even if we wanted to.

The ideal strength training program for runners emphasizes a wide range of exercises for the legs as well as for the upper body, performed with moderate poundage and strict form. With this kind of program, you'll develop a sleek, toned body—not a hulking mass. You'll also achieve something that's important in injury prevention: muscular balance. For every major muscle in the body, there is an opposing muscle. Together, they enable movement to take place. In running, for example, the hamstrings work much harder than their opposing muscle group, the quadriceps muscles of the thigh. So people who just run develop hamstrings that are much stronger than their quadriceps. This kind of imbalance can lead to knee injuries.

How do you achieve muscular balance? By strengthening the entire leg. "The more muscularity you have around a joint," says Scandalis, "the more protection you offer the joint—in this case, the knee." So don't leave out the legs when you plan a strengthening regimen (I'm amazed at how many runners still do). Specifically, use movements—such as squats, lunges, leg extensions, and curls—that will work both the front and back of your leg.

How to Get Strong

Remember the physiological definition of strength: the ability of a muscle to produce force. Resistance training conditions your muscle to produce more force, and resistance training generally means weight training. The best way to build strength is resistance training, hands down.

In 1990, the American College of Sports Medicine added resistance training to its minimum recommendations for fitness, citing some of the muscle-loss studies and injury-prevention benefits mentioned earlier. That means everybody should be doing some form of resistance training at least twice a week. Research strongly suggests that resistance training will not only improve running performance but, more important, will also promote overall fitness by maintaining bone density (an important factor in the prevention of osteoporosis) and muscle mass and helping to prevent lower back injuries. In short, the sports medicine community believes that everybody—and not just bodies named Arnold—should be muscling up. That certainly includes runners, who gain added performance advantages from being stronger.

Another myth about strength training—particularly the kind of training that you and I are likely to do—is that it requires long hours in a gym trying to lift mind-boggling amounts of weight. Not so. "To get the benefits," says strength coach Jamie Nelson, "you need to push yourself, but not kill yourself."

A program of free weights or resistance machines such as Universal, Nautilus, or Cybex is the best way to build strength. But you can start today, at home, with just three basic exercises, using your own body weight as resistance. Do 8 to 15 repetitions of each exercise, three sets each. Breathe rhythmically and move in a slow, controlled manner.

1. *Push-ups*: Great for the chest, shoulders, and arms. Start with the modified version: knees on the floor, ankles crossed. Keep your palms flat, slightly wider than shoulder width. Descend slowly, touching your chest and hips to the floor simultaneously. Push up, pause, and repeat. Once you can comfortably do standard push-ups, make sure you keep your back straight.

2. *Crunches*: This is the proper way to strengthen your mid-section—not the old-fashioned sit-ups, which tend to work your hip flexors more than your abdominal muscles. Lie with your feet up on a chair or flat on the floor, knees bent. Cross your hands over your chest and then raise your shoulders, keeping your lower back flat on the floor. Feel the tension in the stomach muscles, then lower your shoulders slowly and repeat. Exhale as you lift yourself up, inhale as you lower yourself back down.

3. *Squats*: Squats work the total lower body. Consider them as not-too-deep knee bends. Keeping your back straight, your head up, and your hands out in front or at your sides for balance, slowly descend into a seated position. Then push up from your heels, keeping your feet on the floor.

Feel that power in your legs? That's what strength training works to preserve and improve. Try doing three sets of 8 to 15 quality repetitions of each of these exercises, three times a week. As soon as you can, however, I urge

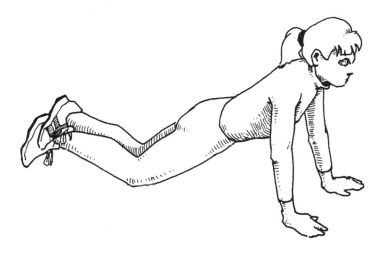

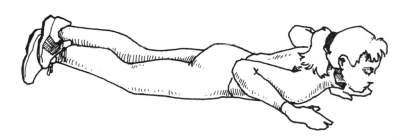

Modified Push-up: With knees on floor, ankles crossed, palms flat and slightly wider apart than shoulder width, descend slowly and simultaneously touch your chest and hips to the floor.

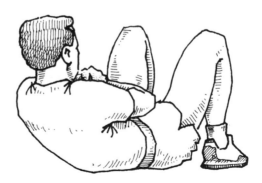

Crunches: Lie on your back with feet on a chair or flat on the floor. Cross hands over chest and raise shoulders. Keep lower back flat on the floor.

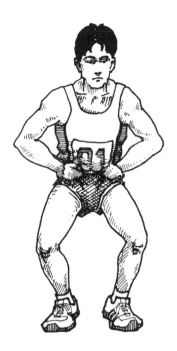

Squats: With back straight, head up, hands out straight or to the sides for balance, slowly descend into a squat position. Keep feet flat on floor.

you to join a health club and get proper instruction on the free weights or machines available there. Or get a pair of dumbbells and an instructional strength-training exercise video.

Whether you do it at home or in the gym, start pumping up. You'll feel the difference in your running—and your life.

CROSS-TRAINING

Triathlons—those swim, cycle, run competitions you may have seen on TV or even in the streets of your town— have become popular over the past decade. The growth of that sport has been fueled largely by runners who ran too much and either got bored or, more likely, injured and were looking for alternative forms of training and alternative competitive goals. I offer this partially as a warning against overtraining. I know that may sound odd, just when you're trying to establish or reestablish a regular training program, but I've seen it happen too often. People get hooked on running—it is often called a "positive addiction"—and start to run every day. Soon they're running significant distances—up to 10 miles or more—day in and day out. That's fine for your cardiovascular fitness, but it's going to lead to only one end: injury.

Although research shows that you need to run at least three days a week to improve as a runner, you don't have to pound the pavement every single day to get the benefits. Indeed, the research also shows that optimal performance is obtained by training four to five days a week. Beyond that, the rate of orthopedic injuries rises.

So what happens on days when there's a blizzard or a torrential rain outside? What happens when the mercury climbs too high for comfort, or the winds howl, or you live in a city and get home too late to run safely? Do you blow off your run? Maybe you have to, but by doing so you're missing a day of cardiovascular training. That is why it's convenient as well as prudent to do some form of cross-training from time to time.

Because cross-training is a term that's thrown around a

lot, I went to the source for a definition: marathoner Gordon Bakoulis' book by the same name. "Cross-training," says Bakoulis, "is any fitness program that incorporates a variety of activities in a systematic way to promote balanced fitness." Of course, that's what you're doing by adding flexibility and strength-training exercises to your running program. But although running may be the best way to develop cardiovascular endurance, it's certainly not the only way. Aerobic cross-training can be achieved by any number of means: cycling, stationary biking, cross-country skiing, aerobic dance classes, rowing, swimming, even walking.

You should do these activities not only to promote cardiovascular fitness—that is, by doing them continuously for 45 minutes at an intensity level that allows you to talk but not sing—but also for your mind, for your body, and certainly for your knees.

TEN COMMANDMENTS
OF INJURY PREVENTION

A study by the Centers for Disease Control in Atlanta revealed that approximately 15 percent of all runners will seek medical attention for some type of injury within a given year. The actual injury rate is probably higher, considering that most runners don't seek medical advice for most minor injuries. When I speak to local running clubs in the New York area, I tell them that based on my experiences and observations, injury is where distance running and pro football have something in common. I think the injury rate is about the same: Nearly 100 percent of all participants suffer some injury at some point in their careers.

Although that may be unavoidable in the NFL, it can be prevented on the roads. How? By keeping your muscles strong and supple and by following some commonsense principles. Many of these have already been touched on; others will be addressed in the next chapter. A useful summary is offered by the International Marathon Medical Directors Association: the "Ten Medical Commandments" for the prevention of injuries in marathon or long-distance running. Abide by these, and chances are you won't be sidelined:

1. Make sure that you are physically fit for the running activities you are undertaking.

2. Train properly.

3. Follow guidelines for proper nutrition.

4. Maintain adequate hydration before, during, and after the race (in other words, drink plenty of water).

5. Perform warm-up and stretching exercises before, and cool-down and stretching exercises after, the run.

6. Dress properly, according to the weather.

7. Use proper, comfortable shoes.

8. Watch the condition of the running surface or road.

9. Don't overdo it; run at your own pace.

10. Listen to your body; slow down or even stop if you do not feel well.

INJURIES AND
HOW TO DEAL
WITH THEM

Mary Ann Stepic, a 26-year-old competitive triathlete who's been running for 12 years and has sustained a slew of injuries, was once told by her orthopedic surgeon to stop running—forever. This is not the advice a runners wants to hear. "He told me I might not be able to run or walk again. He was totally against my running; he was trying to protect me," she says. The doctor advised taking up another sport, which Stepic did, but she simply couldn't shake the desire to run. "I can swim all I want and I'll never hurt my legs or knees, but I didn't want to do only that. I loved running so much that I didn't want to stop."

Luckily for Stepic, her doctor had overstated the seriousness of her condition, but she typifies the mind-set of the runner. A runner runs, as they say, and because of a variety of factors, runners are prone to injury. There's a fine line between pushing yourself to the limit—which is the essence of competitive running—and hurdling over into the injury abyss. You can, however, minimize the extent of your injuries and the amount of running time you'll miss.

This chapter briefly examines the broad spectrum of common running injuries: from causes to early warning signs, from the injuries themselves to how they should be treated and by whom. Keep in mind that not every ailment afflicting runners is addressed, as that discussion would surely fill another book. Only some of the most common injuries are covered. (*Note*: Dehydration, hypothermia, heart problems, and similar disorders are not considered injuries in this overview.)

All running injuries result from one, or a combination, of three causes: improper training, biomechanical problems, and environmental factors. By far the most common cause of injuries is faulty training, which can take several forms. Some of the mistakes routinely made by veterans and beginners alike include overtraining, inadequate stretching, insufficient rest, and using poor judgment when recovering from an injury.

Novice runners are especially vulnerable to the syndrome known as "too much, too soon." Many runners are introduced to the sport by joining a friend—who's usually an experienced runner—out on the roads. Instead of consulting a coach or a book like this and devising a gradual training program suited to their individual needs and abilities, they attempt to jump right in at the friend's pace. This is unrealistic, not to mention potentially dangerous— especially if the beginner is overweight or has been sedentary for some time. (Of course, anyone planning to embark on a training program should first undergo a complete physical examination.) Another perilous practice of novices is to suddenly increase their mileage dramatically. The body has only a certain capacity to adapt. By foregoing the vital stage of letting your body slowly become accustomed to doing mileage, you're placing more stress on your body than it can tolerate. An injury may be lurking around the next bend. So how do you increase your distance without increasing the likelihood of injury? Abide by the ten percent rule: don't increase your weekly mileage by more than ten percent.

Even for conscientious competitive runners who have gradually built up their mileage, there's a limit to how much the body can handle before it begins to break down. "In the dictionary of the runner, there is one word that is missing, and that's 'moderation,'" says Dr. Andres Rodriguez, medical director of the New York City Marathon. "Moderation is extremely important. Training must be moderate and on a gradual basis." Sufficient stretching, as discussed in the previous chapter, is equally important.

Then there's rest—called by some the most overlooked part of training programs. Insufficient rest leads to many overuse injuries. One of the basic tenets of competitive running is never to run hard on consecutive days. A hard-easy regimen allows your traumatized muscles time to recover. Every time you run fast, your muscle fibers are injured. Remarkably, the muscles will heal themselves within 48 hours, if you allow them. If, instead, you run hard two days in a row, you are at much greater risk of tearing the fibers and suffering a long-term injury.

Another part of training is allowing an injury to fully heal before resuming running. This is much easier said than done for most runners. A general feeling of depression usually accompanies a layoff for most athletes. There's an overwhelming anxiety to get back out there. Some poor souls even venture to "run through" their injuries (not a good idea). It will take a lot longer to heal and to get back to feeling 100 percent if you continue to run while injured. Furthermore, by compensating for an injury—usually by making an adjustment in one's running form—often a completely different injury will develop. "Runners are addicted to running and many of them use poor judgment," says Dr. Rodriguez. My motto: Think with your head, not with your feet.

Biomechanical problems, including such abnormalities as overpronation, supination, and leg-length discrepancies, are the second most common cause of all running injuries. Overpronation, an excessive inward rolling of the foot upon striking the ground, is the most common biomechanical factor leading to injury. Likewise, supination, or limited pronation, can also cause injuries. Over pronation and supination can both be corrected with the use of orthotics: These are shoe inserts made of hard plastic or leather that are prescribed by podiatrists to control such abnormal or excessive motions.

As strange as it may sound, some people have a leg-length discrepancy. One leg is actually shorter than the other. It's fairly clear how a leg-length discrepancy would lead to physical difficulties when running. This problem can be corrected with the use of heel lifts.

Finally, the environment—in the form of weather, terrain, and running shoes—can also trigger injury. Running through snow or rain can be a lot of fun, but it can also mean treacherous footing, which translates into injury. There is not much you can do about this, except to be careful.

The same is true for running on slanted or crowned roads (most roads are crowned for drainage; the angle is least pronounced toward the middle of the road), on the beach, or down hills.

Running shoes themselves can cause an injury if they're not well suited to the runner's feet and body type. With the virtually unlimited selection of shoes available today, finding the perfect shoe for you is not so difficult, if you go to a reputable running-shoe store (see Chapter 2). "You have to remember one thing," says Dr. Rodriguez. "The only thing that separates the runner from the road is the shoe. So the importance of shoes is tremendous. If you don't have the proper shoe, you're going to get injured."

You're also going to get injured if you don't pay close attention to the warning signs of imminent trouble. Naturally, experiencing some aches and pains in the muscles, bones, and joints of the lower extremities is to be expected with long-distance running. However, pain that is more serious and persistent should be respectfully acknowledged. When your body signals you about impending danger, you can sometimes avoid an injury. Some pain is rather subtle, so you really have to listen and learn what your body is telling you. When you experience pain while running, you should immediately cut back on your mileage—and possibly stop running entirely for a while. Also, you should never run after taking pain-killing medication, because your body's pain signals will be muted and will subsequently fall upon deaf ears.

Pain isn't the only warning sign, however. The book *Run Gently, Run Long* by Joe Henderson lists 10 others.

1. Low-level and persistent soreness and stiffness in muscles, joints, and tendons.

2. Frequent mild colds, sore throats, and headaches.

3. Swelling of the lymph glands, particularly under the arms.

4. Skin eruptions (acne, cold sores, etc.).

5. Excessive nervousness, depression, and irritability.

6. Nagging fatigue and sluggishness that lingers.

7. Aching stomach, often accompanied by appetite loss.

8. Diarrhea or constipation.

9. Unexplained drops in performance.

10. Disinterest in normally exciting activities.

Corrective action, which usually means cutting back, should be taken immediately after detecting warning signs. If you are unsuccessful in spotting warning signs—or choose to ignore them—you will suffer an injury.

There are two different types of injuries: acute and chronic. Acute injuries, such as a sprained ankle or torn hamstring, are caused by a sudden force; chronic injuries, such as runner's knee and shin splints, develop gradually from repeated trauma. Most running maladies fall into the latter category and are discussed later. For severe acute injuries, first aid may need to be administered. Any bleeding should be stanched, the injured person should be covered to prevent shock, and his or her vital signs should be monitored. Elevate and protect the injured area, and summon medical assistance.

For other acute injuries, all you need to remember is RICE—rest, ice, compression, elevation. Rest should begin immediately to stop the bleeding and swelling of the injured part. For some afflications—muscle soreness, for example—a day or two of inactivity will usually allow the muscles to heal. Ice should also be applied immediately if there is inflammation around the affected area. Ice constricts blood vessels, reducing the blood flow in and around the area, which in turn eases swelling and inflammation. It's recommended to ice the area for 10 to 20 minutes. After the ice is removed, the blood vessels expand and fresh blood flows into the area, bringing oxygen and nutrients and flushing out the damaged tissue. For cases of soreness, strains, sprains, swelling, or inflammation, periodic icing for 10 to 20 minutes for the first 48 hours after the injury occurs is recommended.

Compression further reduces swelling. By wrapping a bandage around the injured area, blood flow to the injured site is restricted. This prevents excess blood from flooding the area (which would cause swelling and inflammation), and consequently directs blood flow from the injury toward the heart, where the blood receives fresh oxygen. It is important, therefore, not to wrap the bandage so tightly that blood flow is entirely cut off. Finally, by elevating the injured area above the level of the heart, you help reduce soft-tissue swelling simply by gravity. RICE is probably the simplest and most effective treatment available to you. Of course, if your injury doesn't respond to RICE within 48 hours or you have other concerns, by all means seek medical intervention.

As alluded to earlier, the runner is a funny creature. Despite the fact that many people run for what they'd term "health reasons," when their health is threatened because of running, they refuse to stop. This is where cross-training is a godsend. Aside from the many benefits cross-training provides in injury prevention, it also enables a sidelined

Cross-Training aids in injury prevention and enables a sidelined runner to maintain aerobic fitness. Bicycling, swimming, and rowing are a few suggested sports for runners interested in cross-training.

runner to maintain aerobic fitness without doing further damage. For practically every injury there is an alternative to running that will not stress it. Nonweight-bearing activities such as bicycling, swimming, and rowing may not give a runner the same satisfaction as running does, but they can certainly chase away depression, lethargy, and fat cells while he or she recuperates. "Cross-training will prevent you from pounding on your heels and on your legs," says

Dr. Rodriguez. "While you're swimming or biking, you're resting the muscles used in running. Therefore, you're able later on to continue jogging."

For a specific running injury, acquiring a proper diagnosis should be your initial concern. Depending on severity and how knowledgeable you happen to be about injuries, you may or may not need to consult a doctor immediately. Naturally, if your pain is intense and you're clueless as to its cause, don't hesitate to see a sports medicine professional right away. If you have a good hunch about what's causing your injury and the pain is tolerable, you may be able to treat it yourself. Obviously, if your home remedy doesn't work, you should then see a professional. Remember to pay close attention to your symptoms so that you can assist your doctor in formulating a correct diagnosis. The following is a sampling of some of the most common running injures, their symptoms, possible causes, and recommended treatments.

RUNNER'S KNEE

DEFINITION AND SYMPTOMS: Runner's knee is actually a catchall phrase that refers to a number of injuries brought on by running. One of the most common ailments is known medically as chondromalacia, or softening of the cartilage, and is basically an erosion of the undersurface of the kneecap. Symptoms of this condition include a "noisy" knee and extreme pain under the kneecap when running long distances, running down hills, or walking down stairs. In addition, a grating sensation can accompany knee movement, and stiffness around the knee may develop after periods of rest.

POSSIBLE CAUSES: Runner's knee is a classic biomechanical overuse injury that can be attributed to myriad factors, including overstriding, overpronation, overtraining, foot or muscle imbalances, leg-length discrepancies, worn-out running shoes, running on slanted surfaces, or incorrect form.

RESPONSE AND TREATMENT: RICE and aspirin (or ibuprofen) to relieve pain and swelling. The affected area should be iced immediately after the injury and after each subsequent run until the pain has dissipated. Training should be reduced and possibly replaced with an alternative activity. Avoid running on roads that are noticeably crowned, as this can cause abnormal pronation. Hill running should be avoided, because it places undue stress on the knees. Exercises to strengthen the quadriceps and promote flexibility in the calf and hamstring muscles should begin right away. Shoes should be checked for improper support, especially in the heels or mid-soles, where the EVA may break down after six months to a year. Orthotics can be very effective in compensating for overpronation, and heel lifts can do the same for a leg-length discrepancy. Finally, arthroscopic surgery—during which damaged cartilage is scraped away through a small incision in the knee —should be considered only as a last resort.

SHINSPLINTS

DEFINITION AND SYMPTOMS: Like runners knee, the term shinsplints is a general one. Basically, it refers to pain in the inner aspect of the lower leg. Shinsplint pain is usually felt upon making contact with a hard surface (such as running on concrete). A sure sign of the injury is feeling pain when the area around the shinbone is touched.

POSSIBLE CAUSES: Shinsplints may have several causes: traumatic periosteitis of the tibia, early minute micro-fractures of the tibia, and sometimes tendinitis or myositis of the lower leg. Shinsplints may be aggravated by over-pronation and tightness in the rear leg muscles. Other possible causal factors include leg-length discrepancies, overtraining, overstriding, improper shoes, and running on slanted surfaces. Shinsplints are especially common among beginning or unconditioned runners who try to do too much too soon.

RESPONSE AND TREATMENT: RICE and aspirin to re-lieve pain and swelling. If the case is mild, usually a day or two of rest will alleviate the condition. In more severe cas-es, mileage should be curtailed and an alternative, non-weight-bearing activity (such as cycling, swimming, or deep-water running with a flotation device) should be con-sidered. Continuing to run through severe shinsplints can lead to serious stress fractures. A return to running should be gradual, and running on banked surfaces should be avoided. Also, a switch to softer surfaces may be advisable. Shoes with good cushioning qualities should be worn; heel lifts can also reduce pressure on the shins. Proper stretch-ing of the hamstring and calf muscles is vital. Orthotics may be prescribed for overpronation.

STRESS FRACTURE

DEFINITION AND SYMPTOMS: A stress fracture is a break of a bone, usually occurring in the feet, shins, or thighs, and sometimes in the ankles or pelvis. It is caused when a bone can no longer withstand increased pressure placed on it. Stress fractures are sometimes difficult to diagnose, especially since regular x-rays are often not sensitive enough to detect them. Stress fractures typically begin as a dull ache that, if ignored, develops into a sharp, excruciating pain. If a spot on the bone hurts intensely when pressed and is accompanied by slight swelling, a stress fracture may be the reason.

POSSIBLE CAUSES: Too much mileage (especially in shoes with inadequate shock absorption), improper running form, foot instability, a sharp increase in mileage or intensity of workouts, improper weight distribution, or a calcium-poor diet.

RESPONSE AND TREATMENT: Complete rest of the injured area is mandatory. All running (except for the deep-water variety) should cease entirely for four to six weeks (sometimes longer). Generally, a cast is not necessary—unless that's what it takes to force you not to run. A nonweight-bearing alternative activity such as cycling or swimming should be started to help strengthen the muscles surrounding the injured bone, and to maintain fitness. Once recovered, be sure to wear shoes with adequate shock absorption, try to run on softer surfaces, and increase your calcium intake if necessary. Furthermore, care should be taken not to overstress one particular part of the body. It should be noted that running through a stress fracture can lead to a larger and much more devastating break in the bone.

ACHILLES TENDINITIS

DEFINITION AND SYMPTOMS: The Achilles tendon runs from the calf muscle to the heel. When too much force is placed on the tendon, microscopic tears result. The initial injury affects the fatty tissue around the tendon, and pain can be felt when the area is touched. If symptoms are ignored, the tendon itself becomes damaged, is replaced with scar tissue, and begins to hurt chronically.

POSSIBLE CAUSES: Overpronation, excessive hill running, tight calf and hamstring muscles, and a shoe with a soft heel counter or insufficient flexibility in the forefoot.

RESPONSE AND TREATMENT: Again, RICE and aspirin are effective treatments. If it hurts to run, you should stop completely and find a nonaggravating alternative activity. Otherwise, running on soft surfaces is recommended. Continuing to run with a torn tendon can eventually lead to a rupture, which is quite serious. Using heel lifts, as well as wearing shoes with firm heel counters and special arch supports, can sometimes rectify the problem. Although stretching the hamstrings is recommended for added flexibility, you shouldn't stretch the calf muscles until all pain has subsided. Stretching an injured tendon will increase the damage. Also, even after recovery, fast and uphill and downhill running should be avoided for a few months.

STRAINS AND SPRAINS

DEFINITION AND SYMPTOMS: A strain simply means that a muscle or connective tissue has become inflamed because of excessive stress. A sprain, which is significantly more severe, is an actual rupture in the tissue. Pain and swelling accompany both conditions.

POSSIBLE CAUSES: Strains can result from sudden bursts of speed when the body isn't ready, running on slippery or uneven terrain, muscle imbalances, leg-length discrepancies, overstriding, hill running, or wearing shoes with uneven wear or inadequate support. Sprains are typically caused by an accident while running, although they can be the result of structural imbalances or running on rough terrain.

RESPONSE AND TREATMENT: RICE and aspirin. In the case of a sprain, you shouldn't run until all pain and swelling have disappeared; adhesive strapping of the ankle and foot will give support and reduce soft-tissue swelling. For strains, you should simply lay off until you can run without favoring the injury. Running on smooth, even terrain is suggested, as is strengthening weak opposing muscles and wearing proper shoes.

PLANTAR FASCIITIS AND HEEL SPURS

DEFINITION AND SYMPTOMS: Plantar fasciitis is an inflammation of the fibrous tissue, or plantar fascia, found beneath the arch of the foot. The condition results from irritation of this tissue and its separation from the heel bone. It is often associated with the presence of a bony spur at the bottom of the heel bone. Pain is usually felt most intensely upon arising in the morning and is usually aggravated by running.

POSSIBLE CAUSES: An unstable, or hypermobile, foot generally causes the overstretching of the plantar fascia. Other potential causes of this injury are tight rear leg muscles or wearing shoes that are too small, have a soft heel counter, or are worn down in the heel.

RESPONSE AND TREATMENT: Good old RICE and aspirin again. As with most of the other injuries described so far, anti-inflammatory medications can be prescribed too. Massage can also be effective. Running on softer surfaces or finding an alternative activity is helpful. For more severe cases, all running should cease. Orthotics or taping can relieve strain by raising the arch. Heel lifts or pads help reduce weight on the front of the heel. Stretching the calf and hamstring muscles is also beneficial. The very last resort in the treatment of this ailment is surgical. The plantar fascia is severed from its attachment on the heel bone, thus decreasing the tension on it.

BACK PAIN AND
SCIATICA

DEFINITION AND SYMPTOMS: Sciatica is a condition in which pain is felt along the course of the sciatic nerve, which runs all the way from the lower back to the foot. Sciatica can take the form of either a numbing sensation or a severe shooting pain. It may be felt anywhere along the nerve, including the back, hip, leg, ankle, or foot. Regular lower-back pain in runners is often accompanied by muscle strains or spasms.

POSSIBLE CAUSES: A veritable smorgasbord of factors can lead to back pain or sciatica. Some of these include a herniated intervertebral disk (or "slipped disk"), an acute lower-back sprain, misalignment of the spine, and overtraining.

RESPONSE AND TREATMENT: Rest is essential. Anti-inflammatory oral medications and muscle relaxants relieve muscle spasms. A lower-back support, or lumbosacral corset, is most beneficial. You should stop running until the pain has dissipated, and then gradually resume your activities. You shouldn't stretch the injured area until you're pain-free. Corrective exercises can then be implemented. Severe cases of back pain or sciatica require medical attention. If left unchecked, the problem will probably lead to a chronic and disabling condition. As a last resort, surgery can be performed to remove or fuse ruptured or damaged disks.

FINDING A DOCTOR

If you've decided to seek medical assistance, there are a number of avenues you can pursue. In fact, with the recent revolution in sports medicine, choosing a specialist can be confusing. Word of mouth is generally a reliable way to find a specialist. Because almost all runners become injured at some point, there are plenty of people you can ask for referrals. Additionally, your family physician can point you in the right direction. Or, if you prefer, you can go to a privately run sports medicine clinic, where a variety of specialists work under one roof. Running clubs are often another good source for referrals (see next chapter). In case none of these options suits you, the phone numbers provided below can be called for referrals.

Naturally, the specialist you see will be determined by the type of injury you've sustained. Dr. Rodriguez suggests, "If your injury is in the foot, you should see a podiatrist who handles sports injuries. If your injury is a musculoskeletal one, you should see an orthopedist or a physical therapist." The following is a short list of some of the different types of sports medicine professionals and how to find them.

Osteopaths: Osteopathic medicine is not a specialty but rather, a broad, comprehensive approach to medical care, with an emphasis on prevention. D.O.s (doctors of osteopathy) are represented in all of the medical specialties; for a list of the ones nearest you—and those who would be most likely to treat a running-related injury—call the American Osteopathic Association in Chicago (312-280-5800).

Orthopedist: An orthopedist is a medical doctor who specializes in musculoskeletal disorders of the joints and bones. An orthopedic surgeon can obviously perform surgery. If you suspect that your injury is structural or possibly a fracture, you should see an orthopedist. A list of orthopedists in each state is available from the American Orthopedic Society for Sports Medicine at 708-803-8700.

Podiatrist: A podiatrist is a medically trained foot specialist (though not an M.D.). In most states, podiatrists are limited to treat injuries below the ankle. Aside from utilizing treatments such as taping, ultrasound, and whirlpool therapy, podiatrists can prescribe orthotics (which, incidently, can sometimes correct problems occurring above the ankle). To locate a sports podiatrist in your area, call the American Academy of Podiatric Sports Medicine at 301-424-7440.

Physical Therapist: A physical therapist is a health professional who usually works in tandem with a doctor. (In most states, a physical therapist cannot treat you unless you are referred by a doctor.) Physical therapists use various techniques to reduce joint stiffness and speed healing, and they teach therapeutic exercises to patients. You can find a sports physical therapist by calling the American Physical Therapy Association at 800-285-7787.

Chiropractor: Certified chiropractic sports physicians use physical manipulation and spinal adjustment to treat injuries—mainly overuse injuries caused by biomechanical imbalances. For referrals, call the American Chiropractic Association Sports Council at 800-593-3222.

Other specialists: These include acupuncturists, accupressure specialists, and sports massage therapists. Once again, what you're seeking from a specialist is diagnosis and treatment options. If an orthopedist recommends surgery as treatment, you should always get a second opinion. "Surgery is something you do as a very last resort," says Dr. Rodriguez. He candidly admits that unnecessary surgery does happen. Obviously, it's important to find a sports medicine professional you trust or who comes well recommended. Also, as Dr. Rodriguez points out, "You should go to a doctor who has experience in dealing with runners."

In the final analysis, the runner's best defense against injury is common sense. Taking the appropriate measures to avoid injury in the first place is of paramount importance. You should also strive to correct any training or biomechanical irregularities you may have or develop, and use caution when facing environmental hazards. If a pain develops while you're running, listen to it! Stop and curtail or discontinue running for a while. If you actually become injured, immediately cease running and allow your injury to heal by finding an alternative activity that doesn't aggravate it. If your injury doesn't respond to rest (RICE, in most cases), you should seek medical attention. It's a fairly simple strategy, but it can pay huge dividends, enabling you to do what you love most: run.

As for Mary Ann Stepic, the triathlete who would rather risk incapacitation than give up running, through trial and error—and injuries—she has developed a thorough knowledge of just how much stress her body can tolerate. "I center my workouts around preventing injury," she says. "That's always on my mind." Her routine includes ample stretching, cross-training, and never running hard on consecutive days. And, I'm happy to report, as this book goes to print, she's still walking—and running!

HOW TO KEEP IT UP,
KEEP IT SAFE, AND
KEEP IT FUN

"I've been running now for over 20 years," says Mike Polansky, a corporate attorney and president of the Plainview–Old Bethpage (N.Y.) Road Runners Club. "And I don't think I'd still be at it if I had run alone. There are times when you want to run by yourself, but not every time."

To be fair, I know lots of runners who have run alone for years. If you're in a job where you're surrounded by people all day long (or you're a homemaker surrounded by kids!), you may choose to run solo simply to get a few blessed moments of solitude. Still, I tend to agree with Polansky—this notion of the "loneliness of the long-distance runner" just doesn't ring true. Although almost every runner runs alone by either choice or necessity once in a while, it's by and large a social sport. I think this is one reason it has maintained its mass popularity for 20 years.

For years I ran by myself, and sometimes I still do. Al-

6

though I thoroughly enjoy these solo runs, I've derived greater pleasure from the sport since I started sharing the roads with others. I've learned a lot, I've made some great friends, and I've found that those friends provide an effective motivational technique. It's called guilt.

Polansky explains: "Back in the mid-1970s, a bunch of us would get together every morning to run at 5 A.M.," he says. "Now it's one thing to get up at 4:30 when it's just you. But when you know there are three other guys waiting for you, it's different. If you're scheduled to run with someone else, you're less likely to just bag it and go back to bed."

So how you do find a running partner? Start by asking around. Maybe there's a friend, neighbor, or coworker who'd like to get started in a running program. Or you could check at your local running-shoe or sports-apparel store or health club. Many of them have bulletin boards or partner-matching services. If you still need help or you're new to an area, you can call the American Running and Fitness Association's Workout Referral Service (the number, in Bethesda, Maryland, is 301-897-0198).

One of the best things you can do is join the 108,000 other runners who have become members of their local running clubs. There are about 450 of them in the United States, ranging in size from the 11-member Deridder Road Runners Club of Deridder, Louisiana, to the 29,000-member New York Road Runners Club (for the one nearest you, call The Road Runners Club of America). Polansky's club, the 1,000-member Plainview–Old Bethpage Road Runners Club, is a great example of how such groups can help keep people involved with and excited about their running. Every Saturday and Sunday, the club has group runs of varying distances and at varying paces. There are mapped out, measured courses, so the runners know just how far they're going. And if you get in with a chatty bunch of runners, you'll find that the time flies as you discuss everything under the sun—including running. "One of my friends and I have solved all the world's major problems during our runs," says Polansky. "We solved Northern Ireland, Palestine, and we just finished Yugoslavia. It all seems so easy on the roads." So does running—when you've got someone to share the road with.

HOW TO RUN SAFELY

Because of different schedules and different lifestyles, every runner will inevitably find himself or herself running alone on occasion. And although this is not advisable as a steady diet, it certainly has its mind-clearing benefits. Polansky and his running buddies may solve the problems of the world during their runs, but solo runners often tell me that they solve their own problems as they cover the miles.

Running by yourself can also lead to problems, though, if you're not careful. Let's start by focusing on one particular area of potential trouble for runners—traffic. In case you haven't noticed, motor vehicles outweigh and outnumber you, and they have the right of way, too. So to help make sure your next run (or even your first run) isn't your last, remember these commonsense precautions:

❦ Run defensively. That's hard to do when you're cruising along on a beautiful day or lost in thought, so stay alert and keep your eyes open—especially when traffic is approaching. "If possible," suggests Andrew Mulrain, a runner and deputy police chief in Nassau County, New York, "ascertain if you have eye contact with the driver of an approaching vehicle. Then you can see where he's looking, and whether he's aware of you."

❦ Obey traffic signals. Yes, runners are subject to traffic signals too. So remember your license test: Green means go, red means stop, yellow does not mean speed up.

❦ Always make the first move when a car is coming toward you. Don't expect the car to move, and don't challenge or play chicken with the car. I'll say it again: Cars are bigger and stronger than you are, even if you lift weights.

❦ Always wear reflective or light-colored garments in the morning or at night, so drivers can see you easily. As I said in Chapter 2, a reflective vest costs just a few dollars, and it's an investment that could literally save your life.

❦ Use shoulders and sidewalks when possible, but if you have to run in the road, face the traffic. "At night, it's a lot easier to see headlights than taillights," Mulrain notes. Day or night, facing traffic as you run gives you advance warning of approaching cars, and it gives the drivers an opportunity to see you.

❦ Be careful of stopped cars waiting to make a right turn into traffic. Either stop and wait, or go *behind* them.

❦ Beware of blind driveways and alleys. People backing out of driveways or pulling out of parking lots have a tendency to blast out halfway into the street before looking for traffic—much less for runners.

❦ Use the crosswalks when running across an intersection. "That's where pedestrians should be going," says Mulrain. "The vehicle operator expects you there."

❦ Don't run in front of cars at stop signs. Between the first and second car is safer. You are more likely to be seen by the driver of the second car, since the first is concentrating on the traffic and not on you.

❦ If you want to listen to music, go to a concert hall. The sound of music on a portable stereo could block out the melodious honk of a car coming up behind you, so don't wear portable headsets. "You're losing one of your senses," Mulrain says. "And you need every sense you have when you're on the roads."

That advice applies even more to the next topic. It would be nice to think that runners could run wherever they chose, without fear of being attacked. Perhaps you're lucky enough to live in a place where it really is safe for a runner—particularly a female—to run alone without worry. Unfortunately, for most of us, that's not the case. Still, there are precautions you can take. "One of the most important things to do is to learn to trust your instincts," says Lisa Gundling of the American Running and Fitness Association (ARFA). "If you're out running and start to feel uncomfortable in your surroundings, don't hesitate to walk or run in another direction."

Gundling also cites an FBI study of 41 serial rapists responsible for 837 attacks, which found that most victims are alone, most are chosen because of their vulnerable location, and most assaults are based not on the individual's appearance but on her availability. Based on this and similar studies, as well as common sense, ARFA, the New York Road Runners Club, the Road Runners Club of America, and other running organizations have compiled lists of tips for personal safety. Here are some of them:

🐾 Do not run alone after dark, especially in parks or isolated areas.

🐾 Do not wear jewelry.

🐾 Carry identification—or at least write your name, phone number, and blood type on the inside of your running shoe.

🐾 Carry a whistle or other noisemaker.

🐾 Once you've moved off the neighborhood track and onto the roads, try to vary your route. When you run, stay in the middle of the sidewalks or (traffic permitting) the street, away from alleys, buildings, and parked cars.

🐾 Be familiar with the area where you run. Stay away from trails surrounded by heavy brush or dense trees. Avoid isolated, unpopulated areas.

The vast majority of runners do not run into problems. Still, you can't ignore the fact that there are risks. Follow these rules, and you'll help minimize those risks.

RUNNING AND DOGS

Another ARFA recommendation for personal safety is to run with a dog. But as they also noted, "there's something about runners and dogs that brings out the worst in both."

Indeed, you may find yourself running with a dog, but it's even more likely you'll find yourself running from one. To keep that from happening, try not to come up on a dog too fast. If you see a dog up ahead who is preoccupied and may not know you're coming, announce yourself while you're still at a safe distance. " 'Are you a good dog?' from a distance of about 50 feet, is a perfectly civil question," writes Trevor Smith in *Running and FitNews*. "If the response is a bark and a wagging tail, things are just fine." If you meet a dog that stands its ground and barks, growls, or snarls, it's probably trying to protect its territory. Don't try to make nice with this pooch—instead, make tracks the other way.

Smith notes that some breeds with a hunting instinct may chase you when you run away from them. This is not necessarily aggressive, he adds; "they'll usually lose interest if they're ignored." Unfortunately, the German shepherd that followed me for 2 miles along a road in rural Connecticut one morning wouldn't lose interest no matter what I did. The dog wasn't hostile. It just seemed like he wanted companionship. But as we crossed a busy intersection, I started to worry less about my safety and more about his. I finally stopped at a local gas station and asked one of the attendants for help. It turned out that they knew the dog and promised to drive him home. I didn't wait around to meet his master, because I would have had some choice words for that person.

If you're a dog owner, you may very well want to run with your dog. Lots of people do. Dogs are good company and possibly good protection as well. But remember: Not all dogs can handle a running regimen.

"A dog's physical condition, age, breed, weight, and responsiveness to basic obedience commands such as heel, sit, stay, and no should all be considered before a regular jogging routine is established," David M. Bebiak, director of pet nutrition and care research of the Purina Pet Care Center. "The first step in setting up a regular exercise program for your pet is to see a veterinarian to ensure that the dog is healthy and able to sustain the workout." Once you've got the green light from your vet, apply the same lessons you've learned about beginning a running regimen to your dog. That is, be conservative and add mileage gradually. Bebiak recommends that you start with 5-minute walks or runs three times a week for the first couple of months and increase the distance slowly. "If your pet begins to lag behind while you're jogging, slow down or stop to let your pet rest, because it's becoming overexerted."

Do not feed your dog sooner than four hours before or one hour after a strenuous workout. Water intake should also be controlled. That doesn't mean that water should be denied, but it should be provided in small amounts rather than allowing the dog to gulp while it's panting.

Here are some other tips on running with a four-legged buddy:

❦ No matter how well-disciplined your dog is, keep him on a short leash while running. He's vulnerable to cars, bicycles, and other unleashed animals if you allow him to roam. He can also scare other runners who don't know that your dog won't bite them.

❦ In hot weather, give your dog a break. You may want to shorten your runs or leave him home altogether. Remember that dogs can get heat stress too.

But they can't tell you when they need water, shade, or rest.

❦ You've got shoes to cushion and protect your feet. Your dog doesn't. So be sensitive to the terrain you're running on: Hot cement can burn a dog's footpads; rocks or rough ground can cut them. Make sure you rinse and dry your dog's footpads after a winter run on sidewalks that have been salted or treated with chemical ice removers. They can burn or even poison your dog if he licks them off.

GETTING MOTIVATED ON
COLD WINTER NIGHTS

It's cold, its' dark, you have a headache from sitting in front of your computer screen all day or from driving your kids to piano lessons and baseball practice, and your favorite soap or sitcom is cued up and ready to play. What's the last thing you want to do? Run. What's the first thing you should do? Run.

How do you do it? Easy: Stop thinking and start doing. "There's never a shortage of excuses for not exercising, especially in winter," says sports psychologist Jonathan Katz. "The key is that before you have a chance to talk yourself out of it, take action. Start changing into your running clothes. Start stretching. You can keep bitching and moaning when you're outside—but once you're out there and warmed up, you'll feel better."

You can help motivate yourself by recalling all the good things that will happen as a result of your exercise efforts. "In winter, you can come up with 10 good reasons not to exercise, and you'll end up in bed," says Katz. "But it's just as easy to come up with 10 reasons that you should exercise. And then you'll do it." I'll come up with three for you: You'll feel better. You'll look better. And you'll be able to enjoy an extra plate of pasta for dinner.

If you've already experienced the benefits of exercise, keep them in mind. "Provide yourself with a past scenario when your energy was high and the workout was good," says Katz. And, of course, try to make it fun. Some sports psychologists recommend that you try to focus on "performance" versus "outcome" goals. In other words, tell yourself: "I'm going to run 3 miles three times this week." You have control over that. Don't say: "I'm going to fit into that bathing suit by the Fourth of July if it kills me." It just might!

Don't even worry about long-term goals. In the cold heart of winter, just getting through a 30-minute jog is good enough. Don't worry about how fast or how far you go—just go. And don't let yourself talk you out of it. To help silence the couch potato in all of us, here are some snappy rejoinders to negative self-talk:

"It's cold and dark outside. Hand me the remote." You don't want to run outside at night? So work out indoors, or try to enjoy the winter. "I love running on cold winter nights, " says Larry Davidson. "The crispness of the air, the different sights and smells—it really heightens your senses."

"I'm too depressed. Hand me the cookie jar." Exercise can help alleviate that winter depression. And it's helpful for appetite control as well—not to mention a way to burn up calories so that you can eat a bit more than if you didn't run.

"I'm too tired. Hand me a pillow." Get up! A 30-minute

jog through the neighborhood before dinner will reenergize you and help you sleep better when it is time to go to bed.

Sometimes, when all else fails, you just have to tough it out. When I asked Mike Polansky, the 20-year veteran, how he dealt with running in the rain, he laughed and replied: "What rain?"

7

EATING FOR
YOUR LIFE

Runners of all shapes and sizes face the question: Do I eat to run or run to eat? And all of them eventually come up with the same answer: both. Considering his disciplined exercise regimen, President Bill Clinton could probably jog off the jokes about his girth if he didn't use the counter of a local burger joint for a finish line.

You will soon notice how difficult it becomes to run after eating junk food and how smoothly you glide along the road when you're eating well. What follows is not a complete treatise on nutrition and running—that would take up an entire book in itself. Rather, these are the essentials of eating for good living and for good running.

WHAT TO EAT

A balanced diet, as prescribed by the USDA's food guide pyramid in 1992—the long-awaited replacement for the four food groups, which was the dominant meal model for half a century—will require a change for everyone. But this is an important change to make, whether you're running or wearing out the sofa. The health of everyone in your household will improve by following these new guidelines.

Many people who have shifted to this plant-based diet are amazed by the sheer volume of food they now eat. We now know that carbohydrates are not fattening; fats are fattening. A mound of linguini with tomato sauce and a heap of vegetables or salad, accented by a couple of pieces of lean meat, can be a sumptuous meal.

You don't need to be a prisoner of your kitchen to eat well. Many people find that they can prepare enough food on Sunday afternoon to keep them eating wisely throughout the week. Magazines and new cookbooks are packed with recipes that anyone can make in very little time. And chefs and restaurateurs across the nation are heeding the pyramid guidelines.

Carbohydrates

At the base of the pyramid, the widest part, is the bread, cereal, rice, and pasta group—the carbohydrates. Even sedentary people are best-served by eating more carbohydrates, but they're especially important when you're in training.

Now that you'll be running regularly, your body will be asking for new sources of fuel. Your muscles will demand glycogen for energy, a chemical that comes from eating carbohydrates. Glycogen burns easily and efficiently; it's your muscles' favorite meal. But they can't burn glycogen alone without reaching into the larder for some stored fats.

After about an hour of hard exercise, your glycogen will run out and your muscles will make fat their main course.

The trouble is, muscles don't work well on a fatty diet. You get tired and slow and don't recover as quickly. Your muscles want glycogen, and you can find plenty of delicious ways to make both your body and yourself happy by carbo-loading every day. You've heard of marathoners eating mounds of pasta on the day before a race? They're carbo-loading—supplying their muscles with all the glycogen they'll need. Ordinary runners don't have to go to such extremes, but carbohydrates should supply 60 percent of your daily calories.

Whole-grain breads and crackers, pasta, rice, and cereals are terrific and easily accessible sources of carbohydrates, fiber, and vitamins. Choose the least processed, most wholesome products, and check their fat content. And don't defeat the purpose by smothering them with fats. Your muscles are depending on you to supply enough carbohydrates to keep them going strong.

As you talk with other runners, you'll discover that the craving for carbohydrates is common. You'll see them sitting behind stacks of pancakes at breakfast. Check out the finish line at a marathon sometime; tables are piled high with bagels, apples, bananas, and fruit drinks.

Fats

Your biggest enemies are fats, especially animal fats in foods such as butter, cheese, and fatty meats. Although the muscles feed on fat during long workouts, most people have adequate fat stores, and fats are easily obtained by eating a balanced diet.

Fats are burned primarily during low-key activities such as reading and sleeping. "It's not hard to burn fat; we burn it all the time. The sad thing is that fat people burn it less well than fit people," laments Covert Bailey in his best-selling book *Fit or Fat*. It seems unfair, but those who have more fat use fat less efficiently, a downward spiral that makes fat people fatter. The only solution, whether you're fit or fat, is to eat *less* fat.

Our intake of fat should not exceed 25 percent of daily calories. We should avoid saturated animal fats that contribute to heart disease, hypertension, and cancer, and we should limit ourselves to unsaturated fats such as olive and canola oils.

Fish oils provide a safeguard against heart disease through their special chemical properties. Dietitian Nancy Clark, a sports diet expert and marathon runner, advises that you eat at least two or three fish meals per week. Be careful about the manner in which the fish is prepared— choose poached, baked, or broiled without butter instead of fried fish. Canned tuna is an excellent protein source, but you should buy tuna packed in water, not oil.

Sharpen your detective skills to uncover hidden fats. A baked potato is one of the best foods you can eat, but it is commonly smothered with butter or sour cream. A whole-grain roll becomes a turncoat in your war against fat the moment you press butter into it. Distrust package claims of "light" and "low-fat" until you check the small print on the label.

The food industry and restaurants make advances every day to satisfy our palates while reducing fat. Choose carefully. For example, you can find excellent low-fat frozen yogurt with 4 grams of fat per serving to replace your favorite premium ice cream with 24 grams per serving. That's a significant improvement that will make your daily run more pleasant and beneficial.

Protein

If your muscles run out of carbohydrates, proteins can also supply some energy, but their main functions are to build and repair muscles, red blood cells, and hair, and to synthesize hormones. Proteins should account for approximately 15 percent of your daily calories.

Old-time strength-building programs recommended huge amounts of protein to build muscles, but protein alone won't do the job. Why not? Well, building muscle is similar to building a house, and protein serves as the lumber. Dumping it on the construction site won't give you a place to live. Exercise is the carpentry crew, working with the raw materials to build something strong and durable. Without exercise, all you have is a pile of protein. With it, you've amassed a strong structure you can depend on when you're facing the howling winds of fatigue.

Lean meats, poultry, and fish are packed with protein and make excellent complements to high-carbohydrate foods such as pasta and rice. Beans, peas, and lentils are also rich in protein without the animal fats. Eggs are another excellent source of protein. A couple of cups of low-fat milk or yogurt, capped off with 4 to 6 ounces of meat, fish, poultry, or legumes a day, will provide a healthy, active adult with plenty of protein.

When it comes to preparing meat or fish, seek out lean meats, and remove the skin from poultry, then grill, broil, or bake them without adding oils or fats. Marinades made from lemon juice, vinegar, orange juice, soy sauce, garlic, onions, peppers, or herbs naturally tenderize meats and enhance the flavor of fish.

Legumes are eaten as a primary protein all over the world. Add a can of chick-peas or kidney beans to your tomato sauce when making pasta. Lentils are easy to prepare and, like black beans, are wonderful with rice.

If you don't feel like cooking, Nancy Clark stands by peanut butter as a protein that makes a healthy snack or an easy meal when applied to a whole-grain starch. You don't even have to cook to find a convenient source of protein. Any supermarket or deli can provide lean roast beef, turkey breast, or tuna. And you don't need much—3 or 4 ounces at lunch and dinner will do the trick.

By using protein-rich foods as an accent to your meals rather than the focus, you can save money, feel better, and avoid hidden animal fats. If you substitute cheese and eggs for red meat, keep tabs on the fat content. Vegetarians should be careful to compensate for the amino acids provided by animal proteins by combining incomplete vegetable proteins to make them complete. They should also be sure to get the minerals found primarily in meats.

Fruits and Vegetables

Three or four servings of fruit and the same amount of vegetables will stock you up on vitamins C and A, carbohydrates (yes, more carbohydrates), and fiber. Believe it or not, you don't have to walk around with a basket on your head to get all these fruits and juices. Drink a glass of orange juice and cut up a banana for breakfast, and you're on your way.

Bananas, melons, and citrus fruits are nutritionally outstanding and available year-round, as are green peppers and broccoli. When berries, spinach, asparagus, and other fresh produce are in season, dive in and give yourself more variety.

Don't shy away from frozen vegetables and dried fruits. Stock your cabinets and freezer for those times when you can't get to the supermarket or farm stand. Keep a bag of dried fruit in your desk, car, or locker. Hit the salad bars, keeping iceberg lettuce (a nutritional gnat) to a minimum and swerving wide around the creamy dressings, bacon bits, and croutons. Instead, load up on dark green lettuce, spinach, and raw vegetables.

Dairy Products

Your bones are alive, and you need to keep them strong. Both men and women benefit from the calcium in low-fat and nonfat dairy products, reducing the risk of fractures and guarding against muscle cramps and high blood pressure. The best way to get the recommended 800 to 1,500 milligrams of calcium is to have a serving of calcium-rich food with each meal. In addition to calcium, the vitamin D in milk is critical to bone health.

Today, you can enjoy the benefits of milk without its attendant fats. Skim milk and nonfat yogurt are the wispy marathoners among dairy products, and whole milk and regular yogurt are the sumo wrestlers. Skim milk contains 300 milligrams of calcium per cup, and just about anyone can learn to like it. In fact, once you become accustomed to skim, whole milk seems too rich to drink. Two-percent milk presents a misleading proportion (such a small amount!) and is no bargain in the fat category, since whole milk is only 3 to 4 percent milkfat. That's roughly equivalent to two thick pats of butter floating in your glass of milk.

Nonfat yogurt packs 315 milligrams of calcium per cup and provides a delicious base for assembling a fruit-laden dessert. If you find it too tart, add a little honey or maple syrup. Low-fat varieties of cheese are increasingly available. Sprinkle them on a thick pizza crust, top with vegetables to add protein and calcium, and you've made a complete meal.

If you are lactose-intolerant or don't like milk products, eat more leafy and dark green vegetables to boost your calcium intake. Soy milk and the varieties of tofu processed with calcium sulfate are also good sources of calcium, as are canned salmon and sardines.

Ice cream is loaded with fat. Excellent low-fat frozen yogurt is now being made by the same people who introduced America to super-rich ice cream. It's delicious; and the lifesaving difference in fat content is startling.

In her *Sports Nutrition Guidebook*, Nancy Clark dispels some common myths about milk: It does not cause the dry, sticky sensation referred to as cottonmouth; nervousness and anxiety do. It does not cause stomach cramps unless you're lactose-intolerant, but a *lack* of milk or calcium can cause muscle cramps. Finally, drinking large quantities of milk will not mend broken bones faster.

The Keys to Healthful Eating

Nutrition experts agree that balancing the foods in the groups within the pyramid leads to a regimen that will benefit everyone. For instance, eat a bowl of cereal with

USDA's Food Guide Pyramid for 1992

milk and banana for breakfast; for lunch, have a turkey-breast sandwich on whole-grain bread with an orange and a cup of nonfat yogurt; and for dinner, enjoy a thick-crust pizza with tomato sauce and cheese. This is not a meager amount of food.

Whether you are choosing carbohydrate-rich foods or foods from the other levels of the pyramid, your body will benefit most from what Nancy Clark calls the three keys to healthful eating: variety, moderation, and wholesomeness.

Variety ensures that you get a broad spectrum of nutrients unique to each food. Eating one kind of food you've found to be acceptable will eventually bore you. Moderation means that you can occasionally indulge in bacon and home fries for breakfast as long as you eat a low-fat lunch. And wholesomeness is a matter of choosing natural or lightly processed foods. That means apples instead of apple juice, a baked potato instead of potato chips, and whole-wheat bread instead of white bread. Labels that claim "all-natural" don't guarantee anything wholesome.

Warning: Giving up your favorite foods will eventual-ly frustrate you and may send you back to your old ways. Indulge your sweet tooth and cravings occasionally. There's nothing wrong with a little reward; in fact, it can be a good incentive for your first 5-mile run! If you consult the grow-ing number of cookbooks and food magazines converting traditionally fattening recipes into lean treats, you'll find that you can sometimes have your cake and eat it, too.

If you're overweight, abiding by the pyramid and starting a running routine will help you reduce your fat in-take while burning more calories—a combination that's bound to help you take off pounds.

In order to run, first you must walk. One of the most important walks you take is through the aisles of the gro-cery store. Selecting the foods you like best that will most effectively support your active life-style may be a new ex-perience for you. Give yourself a little more time than usu-al. Read labels carefully to detect hidden fats. Choose low-fat versions of everything; if you're disappointed with their taste, you can choose something else next time.

Supplements

Running does not increase your need for vitamins and minerals. It is likely, however, that you will consume more vitamins and minerals due to an increased appetite. A bal-anced diet will give you all the vitamins and minerals you need. If you're intolerant of some important foods, you may need to take a daily multivitamin supplement. Otherwise, unless you feel that you are at risk for nutritional deficiencies, supplements are unnecessary.

It is also unnecessary to increase your salt intake, even if you sweat profusely. The salt tablets doled out by football coaches during hot summer practice sessions have taken their place on the shelf of obsolete medical practices, next to bloodletting and jars of leeches. Most Americans consume three times as much salt as they need in their normal diet. If you're like most people, you would probably benefit from reducing your salt intake.

Fluids

When you're a runner, you are what you drink. The most profound demand running creates in your body is the need for fluids. Failing to drink enough fluids reduces the effectiveness of your blood in transporting glucose to your muscles and flushing out metabolic wastes and by-products. Insufficient hydration will also inhibit your ability to sweat and dissipate body heat.

Getting enough fluids is easy and inexpensive. Forget about warnings that too much water will give you cramps. Experts now agree that you should drink as much water as you comfortably can before, during, and after exercise—especially in hot weather. Anyone can test the adequacy of their fluid intake.

Pay attention to the quantity and color of your urine to find out if you're replacing the fluids you lose. Clear, plentiful urine indicates a normal water balance. Dark, scanty urine tells you to pour on the fluids.

If you are tired and sluggish all the time, with frequent headaches, you could be chronically dehydrated.

This condition, however, is most likely to afflict athletes who exercise heavily in hot weather.

Thirst is a poor indicator of your need for fluids. It motivates you to drink, but quenching your thirst calls for far less liquid than will satisfy your overall physical needs. Slake your thirst, then drink a bit more.

Drink 8 to 16 ounces of water 5 to 15 minutes before you run. This will give you a ready supply for the duration of your daily run. Once you begin to exceed 5–6 miles—or if you're running in extremely hot or humid conditions—you should make provisions for carrying or "stashing" water along the way. Drink another 8 to 16 ounces when you get home. You may have heard that we should all drink eight glasses of water per day. Runners and others physically active people should drink more. If you're urinating frequently, you're probably getting enough.

Water is the ideal drink for hydration. Sports beverages and fruit juices may break the boredom and quench your thirst, but it is unwise to take anything sweet before running. Taken less than an hour before exercise, sugar in soft drinks or even fruit juices gives your muscles a short burst of energy but also sets off the alarm for more insulin to carry the sugar away. The combination of increased insulin and exercise can trigger a hypoglycemic reaction. As you become a more experienced runner, or if you pursue long-distance training or marathoning, you can experiment with replacement drinks. Until then, stick with water. Ordinary water may get boring, so try diluting fruit juice or add a slice of lemon or lime to seltzer.

Maintaining high levels of hydration may be difficult at first, but as you get into the habit of running, it will become second nature.

Caffeine and Alcohol

Caffeine has a dehydrating effect. Otherwise, moderate use of coffee or tea (1 to 2 cups daily) appears to be safe for all but those suffering from ulcers or anemia and pregnant and nursing women. Some runners like the mild stimulation they get from a small amount of caffeine, but coffee and tea are not substitutes for water.

Beer is a legendary favorite among runners, despite the fact that it is a lousy sports drink. Science has improved our knowledge since Jim Fixx noted beer's detriments in his *Complete Book of Running*, then washed down his temperance by honoring beer-guzzling habits.

In the years since Fixx's book, attitudes toward alcohol and training have changed. Beer does contain water and carbohydrates, but the alcohol dehydrates you, causing you to lose rather than replace valuable fluids when you drink it after running. Forget about the carbohydrates in beer. Most of the calories (100 out of 150 in normal beer, and an even higher percentage in "light" beer) are from alcohol, not carbohydrates. And alcohol calories are not converted into glycogen.

Smart beer lovers will quench their thirst with a few glasses of water after running, then enjoy a beer or two later. Other alcoholic beverages are similarly bankrupt in nutritional value.

WHEN TO EAT

"When you get too hungry, you don't care what you eat," warns dietitian Nancy Clark, suggesting that *when* you eat is as important as *what* you eat. Clark advises runners to "fuel up your body during the day. You'll have more energy. And if weight is a concern, cut back at night."

Americans view their evening meal as the main food event of the day. Nutrition experts routinely point out the deleterious effect of this tradition. Few people would consider a donut and a cup of coffee an adequate dinner, but you'd be better off eating that for dinner than making it your breakfast.

A good breakfast stokes your body for the rigors of the day. Follow it with a fully nutritious lunch, and you are either preparing for a well-fed late run or recovering beautifully from your early run. Dinner gives you a chance to relax with your family and fulfill your nutritional needs, but let's face it, you're going to sleep on this meal.

Dinner is not the most important meal of the day, so why worry about spoiling your appetite for it? Nutritious and frequent snacks will help satisfy the demands of the USDA's pyramid and will keep you from getting too hungry. There is nothing sacred about three meals a day.

Eating Before and After Your Run

You want to be comfortable when you run. That means you want to run with a calm, settled stomach without hunger pangs. You also want to prevent the fatigue and disorientation that accompanies low blood sugar (hypoglycemia). And you should have enough fully digested food to provide glycogen to your muscles. Finding the right combination of foods to keep you comfortable may take some time and experimentation. We are all different in this regard. But some rules hold true for the vast majority of runners.

We know that light snacks can be digested within an hour, whereas large meals require 3 to 4 hours for complete digestion. We also know that sweets provide a short-term boost but place a runner in danger of a hypoglycemic reaction. Your stomach must work overtime to digest fatty foods, slowing you down and wearing you out. What's left? Starches and light proteins.

A couple of glasses of water and a handful of wholesome crackers are likely to get you through your daily run. If you don't feel well, skip the crackers next time. Once you find the right snack or the time of day when you feel ready for your run, you will become increasingly familiar with your energy levels and how to adjust them. Maintaining a well-balanced diet will keep your carbohydrate intake high and supply sufficient glycogen to keep you running strong.

Athletes refer to the period after exercise as recovery. It sounds a bit dramatic, but this is your chance to return to your body much of what it spent to carry you home. You've lost fluids, burned carbohydrates, and expended minerals (electrolytes) such as sodium and potassium. Water will replace your fluids. Juices and watery fruits such as watermelon and grapes supply all three: water, carbohydrates, and electrolytes. Sports beverages contain water and carbohydrates but not many electrolytes.

Regardless of what you drink, nothing restores your nutrients like wholesome food. Reach for the carbohydrates again—a bowl of cereal with a handful of raisins or a glass of orange juice with an English muffin. Replace the potassium you may have lost by eating a banana, raisins, yogurt, or a potato or by drinking a glass of orange juice. All these ordinary foods will easily replenish your losses, already preparing you for tomorrow's run.

One of the best features of eating a balanced diet is that you eat the same foods whether you're exercising or resting. You may be hungrier and eating more when you're following a running program, but the foods are the same. Altering your habits to include healthful eating and running will become easier and feel more natural every day.

8

SPECIAL YEARS,
SPECIAL
CONSIDERATIONS

unning is a democracy. Go to any track, park, or road race and chances are you'll see it in action: children and senior citizens, tall and short, skinny and stocky, male and female, rich and poor, college professors and factory workers—all running. Some, like the remarkable people of the Achilles Track Club, have overcome serious illness and physical handicaps. Others have used running as an aid to recover from emotional trauma. Some are leaner, faster, and able to deliver oxygen more efficiently than others; some will never go much faster than my friend Stan Kramberg, who at age 60 and after 15 years on the roads, still runs with a smile—even though he'll probably never run a mile in less than 10 minutes. Some, like you, are running for health and fitness. Others are competitors, running to better a personal time or distance. But despite all those differences, they share one important thing: They're runners. You can be one too. And by now, if you've been following the program, you're well on your way.

For most of us, the transition from sedentary individual to walker to runner can be done, as discussed in previous chapters, with nothing more than your doctor's blessing, a decent pair of shoes, and a dose of common sense and determination. But there are some populations that need to take special care as they begin to run. Their special needs and considerations are what this chapter is all about.

RUNNING AND WOMEN

For women, the question of when to run has another dimension. There are many myths about running and menstruation—the truth is that it's largely an individual decision.

"Some women just won't or can't run during their periods," says Patty Coyle, a top competitive runner in the New York-area, and the cross-country coach for Hofstra University. "My own feeling—and the feeling of many of the women runners I know—is that it actually helps. [Running] gives you more energy, you get rid of a little of the extra water weight. It definitely makes me feel better."

If you're a woman starting a running program, you may find running will help you, too, during your menstruation period.

Can pregnant women run? That was the question posed in an *American Health* magazine article in January 1993. It was about a study done at the Pennsylvania State University College of Medicine, in which researchers compared the pregnancies of 15 veteran runners with those of 35 inactive women. The runners, all of whom had been training at least three times a week for 30 minutes, didn't

THE ESSENTIAL RUNNER

gain as much weight as the sedentary moms-to-be, but they did gain the fat needed to help nurture their developing fetuses. The study went on to track the women and their newborn babies, and found that the running mothers' newborns were an average of half a pound leaner than the babies of the nonrunners. The lower weight wasn't enough to put them at added risk, according to the study's authors, and it helped make delivery easier.

What all this suggests is that the old exercise guidelines for pregnant women—duration no more than 15 minutes, intensity no more than 140 beats a minute—may be too conservative, especially for women who are already involved in a fitness program. Responding to a reader's question in the June 1992 issue of *Runner's World*, Mona Shangold, M.D., offered the following recommendations: "I advise you to continue running at a speed that feels easy to you, slowing or even stopping if you begin cramping, gasping for breath, or feeling dizzy," wrote Shangold, author of *The Complete Sports Medicine Book for Women*. Efforts to increase speed and distance should be avoided. In addition, workouts should be limited to no more than 30 minutes, after which the core body temperature tends to rise.

Despite the restrictions, there are many good reasons why women should run or exercise during pregnancy, or at least until the third trimester. As the Penn State study showed, running can help in weight control. It can also reduce tension, allow for better sleep, and increase energy levels. Keep in mind, however, that most of the findings here are based on the experiences of women who were already fit when they became pregnant. If you're pregnant and thinking of starting a running program, consult your obstetrician or gynecologist.

RUNNING AND KIDS

One of the most memorable events I ever covered as a newspaper reporter was something called "Dinosaur Day." The idea, cooked up by a local running impresario and special-education teacher named Ralph Epifanio, was to hold a running event in which parents and children could participate together. Epifanio knew that the only way to get kids to do anything is to make it fun and give them a little reward for their effort—which is just what he did. I'll never forget the scene of about 500 kids, some just toddlers, with plastic stegosaurus snouts on their noses or pterodactyl wings on their backs, running pell mell across a field toward a 6-foot-tall inflatable tyrannosaurus rex. The kids had a ball, which, as Epifanio noted, was the point. "The important thing here is participation," he said. "Every child gets a prize. We don't want these kids killing themselves."

On the contrary. We want kids to turn off the TV or the video game once in a while and discover the joy of movement and the benefits of exercise. And running is one of the best ways to do that. "I think it's terrific for kids," says Reuben Reiman, a New York City pediatrician and author. "It's a year-round activity. It doesn't require purchasing a lot of expensive equipment. They can do it anywhere and without having to gather up a whole team. And they can do it at their own ability level, without having to compete with anybody but themselves."

Of course, there are precautions you should take. In a 1991 statement, the Committee on Sports Medicine of the American Academy of Pediatrics recommended running, with caveats about the risks connected with training and racing, including overuse injuries and a possible delay in girls' first menstrual periods. They also pointed out that children may take longer than adults to acclimatize themselves in hot and humid conditions.

What this means, says Dr. Reiman, is that parents should apply the same common sense to their kids' running as they do to their own. That means that kids should drink plenty of fluids in hot weather; kids should listen to their bodies as we do: If they feel pain or shortness of breath, they should slow down. And if a pain or problem persists or seems unusual, the youngster deserves a checkup. But, as Reiman points out, the possibility of a child having some congenital heart problem that has not already been detected and might prevent him or her from running is extremely unlikely.

Slightly more common is exertional asthma, which, as the name suggests, may be detected only after a child exerts himself or herself. Even then, Reiman notes, the thinking on that has changed. "Years ago, kids with asthma were made to be sedentary," he says. "Now the feeling is that they should exercise and run. When they've gone as far as they comfortably can, they should pause, and then resume." Not only can children with asthma run, but experience has shown that they can also improve their endurance.

One challenge to parents is motivation. Running does require some effort and a little discomfort at first. So how do you get them to do it? Well, you might try by setting an example yourself. If you're starting a running program, this might be an excellent time to get your kids involved. They'll look and feel better as a result of participating. Another key motivator for kids: Running will help them improve in other sports. "This is something that a kid who is not a great athlete can do on his own," says Reiman, "without people watching him on a playing field. There's no embarrassment in it. And he can even use it as his own sort of 'secret weapon' to improve speed and endurance, which will help him in the other team sports."

One thing parents should avoid is the kind of "no pain, no gain," win-at-all-costs approach to kids sports, often called Little League syndrome. This problem exists in competitive running as well; youngsters, particularly those showing a little talent, are pushed by their parents to run faster and faster, more and more. "A parent who screams his kid into a marathon isn't going to get anywhere," says Reiman. "Except maybe to make that child embittered and turned off toward athletics."

Instead, look for opportunities to get your kids participating with others. More and more road race directors are including kids' fun runs as part of their events. Encourage your kid to do these with you. And make sure that they enter into it in the same spirit as the average adult who runs such races. Do your best, have fun, and be proud of crossing the finish line—no matter what place you finish in.

RUNNING AND SENIOR CITIZENS

Dinosaur Day provoked laughs, but Dr. Paul Spangler inspires awe and respect. Like Max Popper, he's someone who is redefining the notion of aging. Research is beginning to show that much of what has been considered the aging process is really just the result of a lack of exercise, and Spangler is Exhibit A.

Let's put his story in perspective: When Paul Spangler was born, William McKinley was president, and the United States had just fought the Spanish-American War. On December 7, 1941, he was the acting chief of surgery at the U.S. Naval Hospital at Pearl Harbor. On November 5, 1989, when I met him, he was about to line up at the start of the New York City Marathon. He was only 90 then. As this is being written, four years later, he is still running and competing.

As a medical doctor, Spangler understands how running has helped him and how it can help other older adults. "Without any question, I would be dead if I hadn't been active over the last 15 years," says Spangler. "It's enhanced the quality of my life no end. I wouldn't give it up for anything." And the good doctor would like other older Americans to follow his lead. "The quality of life is so much greater," says Spangler. "Once you experience the zest of life that physical fitness has given you, you don't want to give it up. My goal is to be running when I'm 100." He's got a good shot at it. And if he can do it, so can you (and you were probably born *after* the turn of the century).

"In my experience with seniors over the last 10 years, I've found that most can do a lot more than they think they can," says Ellen Coven, a specialist in senior fitness. Coven's forte is aerobic exercise classes for seniors, but much of her advice also applies to those seniors beginning a running program.

Here are a few tips that can help seniors get started on the road to good health and fitness:

❦ Get an OK from your doctor. This is especially important for seniors not only because of medical conditions that may require monitoring or special restrictions, but also because a doctor will be able to allay any fears. "Almost everyone who comes to take a class with me tells me, 'My doctor told me I should start exercising,'" says Coven. "So it seems that more and more doctors are encouraging their patients."

❦ Don't dress to impress: This advice applies to people who are overweight or self-conscious about their appearance as well as to seniors. "In most senior exercise classes, there are no fancy leotards or pants," says Coven. "The main thing is to be cool and comfortable." That advice applies particularly to seniors beginning a running program, as their body temperature can fluctuate more rapidly than that of younger folks. One thing you should bring along is an ID and a medical bracelet, if one is warranted. "Chances are you won't need it," says Coven. "But it's better to be safe than sorry."

❦ Start slowly—very slowly. Hal Higdon, a prolific runner, writer, and author of the *Masters Running Guide*, writes often about running for those over 40. In his book, he offers these tips for a beginner's workout: Exercise easily for 15 minutes. Work up a good sweat, but not too good a sweat. "Particularly for the first several weeks," he writes, "ignore the temptation to measure how far you've gone, or how fast you got there."

❦ Don't go it alone. The local tracks in my neighborhood are filled with seniors walking or jogging together. The same advice offered in Chapter 6 applies to seniors: It's more fun when you do it with a friend.

❦ Finally, in Higdon's words, "forget the past." He's right: Forget about what you could or couldn't do back in high school. Also, forget about the way you may have been trained back then. Although not all training regimens of decades ago were wrong, exercise science has advanced a great deal over the past 25 years. Follow the advice of your doctor, read magazine articles and books such as this one, and build gradually to the point where you may be able to give Dr. Spangler a run for his money.

RUNNING AND SERIOUS DISEASE

I'll never forget the night that Fred Lebow, director of the New York City Marathon, confused me with someone else during an awards presentation. He had a glazed look in his eye; and everybody in the crowded banquet room sensed there was something wrong with Fred—the president of the New York Road Runners Club and one of the most important figures in American running.

There was. Soon afterwards, Fred was diagnosed with lymphoma of the brain. Things looked so bleak that I was asked to write his obituary—just in case.

I did write about Fred. But happily, it was in another context, two years later, when he ran the 1992 New York City Marathon. Accompanied by nine-time N.Y.C. Marathon winner Grete Waitz, some friends, and a few media types (including yours truly), Fred ran the entire 26.2 miles. He did it to help raise money and awareness for cancer and to help inspire other cancer patients. He ended up moving an entire city. The outpouring of affection and support for Lebow along the route was remarkable. Fred finished the race in a time of five hours, 32 minutes; and he showed the world what is possible if you put your mind—and feet—to the task.

Running does many good things for you but, of course, it does not cure cancer. However, a recent survey of members of the American College of Sports Medicine—published in Robert Brody's book "Edge Against Cancer" (WRS Publishing, 1993)—concluded that athletes have a psychological advantage over average people in coping with cancer. And most doctors will tell you that, in almost any kind of illness or injury, an individual in good physical condition has a greater chance of recovery than a sedentary person.

By the way, one of the athletes profiled in the book is Fred Lebow who, as I write this, is running regularly and feeling fine.

MOVING

AHEAD

There's a reason I didn't call this book *The Essential Jogger*. It's because jogging and running are different—although there is some disagreement on exactly what that difference is. Some say it's a matter of speed: Joggers are slow; runners are fast. Some say it's a matter of experience: Joggers are novices; runners are experienced. Others, such as the late George Sheehan, thought the distinction was even simpler than that. "I think the difference is an entry blank," said Dr. Sheehan, the late cardiologist and revered writer on running and fitness. "Once you've been in a race, it changes you permanently."

Of course, you can run forever without racing, if you wish. But at some point, most joggers or runners or whatever you want to call us make the decision to enter a road race. As Sheehan saw it, jogging is a means to an end, that end being weight loss, better appearance, lower cholesterol, or simply being able to fit into the pair of pants you wore on your honeymoon. Jogging depends on willpower—the will to get into the kinds of habits and regimens outlined in this book. But once you've tasted competition, against others and yourself, that all changes. "Instead of willpower, you have want power," said Sheehan. "You now want to do this better. It's not a question of doing it better than someone else. You've established your own criterion; now you want to surpass it."

That implies work, commitment, passion, and something else that you experienced when you first lifted your feet from the walker's gait and attempted to propel yourself around the track: pain. "It's what the Greeks called *agon*," said Sheehan, who, as you've probably gathered by now, had a marvelously philosophical bent. "You have to go into hand-to-hand combat with yourself." Although this may sound very deep—and very uncomfortable—it's really not. "Thoreau made the point that the feelings of pain and pleasure are very difficult to distinguish," said Sheehan. "You suffer during the race, you get through the finish line, and then you feel so good about yourself that you're ready to do it again."

He was right. There may be discomfort along the way, but completing a race is an exercise in self-actualization. Remember the old ads for the U.S. Army, "Be all that you can be"? After a hard race, that slogan takes on a whole new meaning, whether or not you've ever been in uniform. You have worked to the full extent of your ability, and you know it. It's a profound experience, an accomplishment, and, on a more practical level, it's a darn good motivational tool. I once interviewed a guy who had finished dead last in a local triathlon. Why, I asked? "Because the race gives me a goal," he said. "Otherwise, all that training would become a chore, and I'd get sick of it."

You don't have to do a triathlon or a marathon to become a competitive runner, to feel those feelings, to give your training the boost it will probably need at one point or another. You can even use a local 5-kilometer race as a culmination of the beginner's program outlined in this book. Don't worry about your time or about how many people finish ahead of you. I'd almost be willing to bet the cost of this book that you won't be the last person to finish the race. And even if you were, so what? Your first race is not the place to worry about speed. You should be more concerned with finishing strong, feeling good, and having fun.

If you do have the urge to test yourself in a race, there is an intelligent way to do it: "negative splits." This means that you start out conservatively and try to pick up speed with each mile or "split." For a veteran racer, that might be a mistake, but for a novice, I think it's a good way to run a race—and the best way to feel at the end of it.

There are other good reasons for entering a road race. They're relatively inexpensive—entry fees are generally about $12 to $15—and money usually goes for a good cause, such as a local charity. Plus you get the runner's most important item of apparel other than shoes: a race T-shirt, which you can wear with pride after the race. Above all, there's the ambience. "There's a certain energy about a race," said one runner I know. "It makes running more exciting." He's right. Races hum with electricity and excitement. They're also pleasant social gatherings, where friends meet and friendships are made. Indeed, some would say that the party atmosphere and camaraderie of a road race are what brings them out in the first place.

Training seriously for competition means changing your running program. You won't want to go out and simply do the same 3 or 4 miles at the same pace three or four days a week. You'll need to do "overdistance" training; that is, going further than the race distance in training in order to build your aerobic base. You may want to do some hill repeats to strengthen your legs. And many coaches now recommend something called anaerobic threshold running, where you run hard enough to the point that your body produces lactic acid. And don't forget good old-fashioned fast running—speed work—on the roads or on the track.

It sounds onerous, and sometimes it is. But if you want to go far and fast in this sport, these are the kinds of things you need to do. The rewards, I think, are well worth it. Improvements may be gradual or rapid, depending on the individual, but most runners tend to reach their racing peak years after they start. This means that you have something to look forward to: faster times and better performances as you get older. One of the amusing aspects of racing is the eagerness with which runners approach the major birthdays that most people dread. Age categories for races are usually grouped in five-year increments, so a runner turning 50 can look forward to being the youngest—and, theoretically, the swiftest—in the 50–54 age group at local races.

Training for serious competition is the point where this book leaves off. But there are many other books out there that can serve as useful guides. Two of the best author-coaches are Jeff Galloway and Bob Glover, whose books are listed in the bibliography. If you decide to get serious about your racing—now or in the future—I recommend that you consult them. You'll also find good information on races and training in *Runner's World* and *Running Times* magazines.

In the meantime, I don't want to give you the impression that you can't enjoy running by yourself or noncompetitively with friends. You can. After all, even the most driven competitive runners usually race only on the weekends. The other days they do what all runners do: We run and appreciate its simplicity, its accessibility. We savor the time outdoors, alone with our thoughts or together with friends. We thrive on the sense of mental and physical well-being it produces. We revel in the sheer enjoyment of the most natural and basic of all sports. This is the essence of running. Good luck with yours.

APPENDICES

SAMPLE RUNNING PROGRAM

The following program is designed to help the beginning runner get started in the sport. The schedule starts off with walking only. The purpose is to increase your cardiovascular fitness while slowly adapting the muscles to exercise. Starting at week three, easy jogging is interspersed with walking. Remember that the first five minutes of walking is a warm-up. Start slowly and build up gradually. When you first start to run, do not worry about your speed. The important thing is to get comfortable with the movement and to have some fun without getting frustrated or injured.

Around the eighth week, I suggest running on a track to gauge how far and how fast you are running. Keep in mind, however, that your pace will vary according to your fatigue level, the weather, the terrain, and other factors. A conversational pace should be your goal. In other words, you should be able to maintain a conversation without gasping for air.

You will notice that there are many off-days in the program. I suggest that you use these to do some strength training or stretching.

After the fourteenth week, you can add five minutes a week to your longest run. At this stage, you might want to try running on two consecutive days and taking the third day off. One of the runs should be a harder effort followed by a relatively easy run; this is for recovery purposes. For example, on Monday run 45 minutes, followed by a 30-minute run on Tuesday. Then take Wednesday off. This pattern then continues on Thursday and Friday. When you have built up to running for 60 minutes, a new journey can begin: the 10-kilometer (6.2 mile) run. At this point, you may want to test your new-found fitness in a local road race.

WEEK	MONDAY
1	Walk 20–30 Min.
2	Walk 30–45 Min.
3	Walk 5 Min. and Run 3 Min., (3 Times), Walk 5 Min.
4	Off
5	Walk 5 Min., Run 8 Min., Walk 3, Run 8, Walk 3, Run 5, Walk 5
6	Off
7	Walk 5 Min., Run 12 Min., Walk 3, Run 12, Walk 3, Run 12, Walk 5
8	Off
9	Walk 5 Min., Run 18 Min., Walk 2, Run 18, Walk 2
10	Off
11	Off
12	Walk 5 Min., Run 30 Min., Walk 5 Min.
13	Off
14	Off

WEEK	TUESDAY
1	Off
2	Off
3	Off
4	Walk 5 Min., Run 5 Min., Walk 3, Run 5, Walk 3, Run 5, Walk 5
5	Off
6	Walk 5 Min., Run 10 Min., Walk 3, Run 10, Walk 3, Run 10, Walk 5
7	Off
8	Walk 5 Min., Run 15 Min., Walk 2, Run 15, Walk 5
9	Off
10	Walk 5 Min., Run 20 Min., Walk 1, Run 10, Walk 5
11	Walk 5 Min., Run 25 Min., Walk 1, Run 10, Walk 5
12	Off
13	Walk 5 Min., Run 35 Min., Walk 5 Min.
14	Walk 5 Min., Run 40 Min., Walk 5 Min.

WEEK	WED	THURS	FRI	SAT	SUN
1	Walk 20–30 Min.	Off	Walk 20–30 Min.	Off	Walk 20–30 Min.
2	Walk 30–45 Min.	Off	Walk 30–45 Min.	Off	Walk 30 Min.
3	Same as Mon.	Off	Same as Mon.	Off	Same as Mon.
4	Off	Same as Tues.	Off	Same as Tues.	Off
5	Same as Mon.	Off	Same as Mon.	Off	Same as Mon.
6	Off	Same as Tues.	Off	Same as Tues.	Off
7	Same as Mon.	Off	Same as Mon.	Off	Same as Mon.
8	Off	Same as Tues.	Off	Same as Tues.	Off
9	Same as Mon.	Off	Same as Mon.	Off	Same as Mon.
10	Off	Same as Tues.	Off	Same as Tues.	Off
11	Off	Same as Tues.	Off	Same as Tues.	Off
12	Off	Cross-Train	Same as Mon.	Off	Same as Mon.
13	Off	Same as Tues.	Off	Same as Tues.	Off
14	Off	Same as Tues.	Off	Off	Same as Tues.

OTHER SOURCES OF
INFORMATION

National Running Magazines

Runner's World
For subscription information, write P.O. Box 7307, Red Oak, IA 51591-0307, or call 800-666-2828.

Running Times
For subscription information, write P.O. Box 511, Mt. Morris, IL 61054, or call 800-877-4502.

National Running Organization

Road Runners Club of America
629 South Washington St./Suite 250
Alexandria, VA 22314
(703) 836-0558

An association of running clubs. Call or write for information about ones closest to you. Also publishes a quarterly newspaper, "Footnotes," and various other booklets and pamphlets about running.

American Running and Fitness Association
4405 East-West Highway
Bethesda, MD 20814
1-800-776-ARFA

A membership organization of runners and people involved in fitness. Publishes a monthly newsletter "FitNews"; also offers special services, such as running partner match-up and a Running Trials network, providing runners with maps for over 250 cities throughout North America, showing top places to run.

BIBLIOGRAPHY

Anderson, Bob. *Stretching*. Bolinas, Calif.: Shelter Publications, 1980.

Averbuch, Gloria. *The Woman Runner: Free to Be the Complete Athlete*. New York: Cornerstone Library/Simon and Schuster, 1984.

Baily, Covert. *Fit or Fat*. Boston: Houghton Mifflin, 1977.

Bloch, Gordon Bakoulis. *Cross-Training: The Complete Training Guide for All Sports*. New York: Fireside/Simon and Schuster, 1992.

Clark, Nancy. *Sports Nutrition Guidebook*. Champaign, Ill.: Leisure Press, 1990.

Fixx, James F. *The Complete Book of Running*. New York: Random House, 1977.

Galloway, Jeff. *Jeff Galloway's Complete Book on Running*. Bolinas, Calif.: Shelter Publications, 1984.

Glover, Bob, and Pete Schuder. *The New Competitive Runners Handbook*, 2d ed. New York: Penguin Books, 1988.

Higdon, Hal. *Masters Running Guide*. Van Nuys, Calif.: National Masters News, 1990.

Lebow, Fred, Gloria Averbuch, and friends. *The New York Road Runners Complete Book of Running*. New York: Random House, 1992.

Nokes, Tim. *The Lore of Running*. Champaign, Ill.: Leisure Press, 1991.

Shangold, Mona. *The Complete Sports Medicine Book for Women*. New York: Simon and Schuster, 1985.

Sheehan, George. *Running and Being: The Total Experience*. New York: Simon and Schuster, 1978.

INDEX

THE ESSENTIAL RUNNER